This item is due for return on or before the last date below.
It may be renewed by telephone, in person or via the internet at
https://librariesnl.northlan.gov.uk if not required by another borrower.

supported by

First published 1997
Revised 2006
New Edition 2015

Other titles by Hamish Brown
The Mountains Look on Marrakech
Three Men on the Way Way: A Story of Walking the West Highland Way
The Oldest Post Office in the World and other Scottish Oddities
Hamish's Groats End Walk: One Man & His Dog on
a Hill Route through Britain & Ireland

All cover pictures can be found in the book.

Opposite page: At the Almond Aquaduct in olden times

CANALS ACROSS SCOTLAND

Walking   Cycling   Boating   Visiting

The Union Canal
The Forth & Clyde Canal
Country Parks
Roman Wall

HAMISH BROWN

WHITTLES PUBLISHING

Published by
Whittles Publishing Ltd.,
Dunbeath,
Caithness, KW6 6EG,
Scotland, UK
www.whittlespublishing.com

© 2015 Hamish Brown

ISBN 978-184995-162-3

Pictures from the Hamish Brown/University of
St.Andrews Library Collections

Printed by Gomer Press

CONTENTS

FOREWORD

History has bequeathed to the Scottish people some extraordinary public assets, but not one of these comes close in terms of scale or diversity of opportunity to our publicly owned network of canals. Built as a transport network during the industrial revolution, allowed to decline throughout much of the 20th century, they are now enjoying a remarkable renaissance. That they are doing so owes much to the vision and enthusiasm of a small number people who have recognised their contemporary relevance and the huge opportunity that these waterways and towpaths represent.

I am one of thousands of people who have been fortunate to discover the canals in recent years. More are being added to that number every month. Ramblers, long distance walkers, runners, cyclists, boaters, canoeists, bird watchers, fishermen and many others can now be found every day of the week enjoying their canals and deriving immense value from the modest amount of public money that contributes to their upkeep. As those numbers grow so too do the resources available for the canals, allowing better towpaths, more moorings, canal-side cafes and much more to develop.

This excellent guidebook builds on and updates previous editions to reflect that rapidly changing picture. It will be invaluable to canal users, and a delight to those who prefer to enjoy them from afar.

Andrew Thin
Chairman, Scottish Canals

The Falkirk Wheel

PREFACE

This book is written for the entertainment and practical benefit of walkers, cyclists and boaters on the Union Canal (UC) and the Forth & Clyde Canal (F&CC).

Visitors, from those walking the full length of the canals to those spending just a day in a specially interesting area will benefit from its information, its knowledgeable descriptions and good stories. The canals can be enjoyed at any season. In winter, with the trees leafless, the views are more extensive (perhaps to snowy mountains), and offering an alternative when weather rules out hillgoing – and there is less traffic on towpath or waterway. In high summer the green world of trees is almost overwhelming, the banks crowded with sweet reed grass, meadow sweet, willowherbs, vetches and many spreads of yellow waterlily, a real *Wind in the Willows* world. In autumn there are brambles to be eaten; in spring the returning wildlife spree, with swans nesting and swallows swooping. The canals are 'a good thing' at any season.

One thing which often surprises those discovering the Lowland canals, whether on water or towpath, is just how overwhelmingly *rural* the experience is, even within city bounds. The canals are a scenic treat and will repay many visits or provide a dedicated holiday challenge.

The canals are described with some detail but there are also what could be called side trips which deserve exploring (there aren't all that many pubs or cafés on the towpath!). One might forsake the canals' forever flatness to take a day over the Antonine Wall on Croy Hill or Bar Hill, or to some of the country parks or explore places like Linlithgow, Falkirk, Kilsyth or Kirkintilloch, often by circular walks. All this is described. The canal is for leisurely, timeless exploring, and certainly will lead to future returns by car, bus or train to show others what was discovered and to extend experiences. The Falkirk Wheel or the Kelpies will be far more treasured if the first serendipitous experience of them came by or on the canals. Much of my revisiting everywhere for this new guide entailed using a combination of cycling or walking a length of canal and then staying overnight or returning to my van by bus or train or arranging pick-ups from friends. The canal is continuously within easy reach of good bus and train services, both in rural and city locations. Nothing however beats doing Edinburgh to Glasgow as a continuous journey, and with so many towns and good transport links this can be done easily. So, do take *time* and take side trips as well as enjoying the canals – a mixing of opportunities and not just the ever-present towpath in view. Make it special. There really are plenty of pubs and cafés accessible nearby but some may be closed on Mondays; take some liquid and nibbles along.

Introduction

Background History

Much about canals in general, and specific features in particular, appears in the main text, but a few comments may be of interest here. In the canals' heyday during the early nineteenth century, the lack of locks on the Union Canal allowed travellers a speedy crossing between the cities of Edinburgh and Glasgow. The once-thriving service took as little as 13 hours, and cost the equivalent of 7½ pence. At one time there were plans to run the canal through Princes Street Gardens in Edinburgh and down to Leith docks, but fierce opposition blocked this extension.

The concept and planning of the canals was marked throughout by dissension. The Forth & Clyde Canal opened in 1790 and the Union Canal in 1822, but, with an inter-city railway opening as early as the 1840s, they then began a century of decline. Only just in time was their amenity and recreational value realised, with various enthusiastic bodies, local authorities and Scottish Canals (British Waterways Scotland) finally receiving the fantastic Millennium funding that had both canals open and working again. What an impossible dream that would have appeared in 1970.

The Forth & Clyde Canal had started at Grangemouth in 1768 (it was only fully opened in 1790, as funds kept running out during construction) and this is often claimed to be the first canal cutting in Scotland, a fact which, as a Fifer, I cannot let pass unchallenged. The first canal known in Scotland was at Upper Largo, when the great naval hero Sir Andrew Wood (c.1455–1539) had some of his captive English crews cut a canal from Largo House to the local kirk so he could be rowed to church in his admiral's barge – at the end of the 15th century.

The first proposal for a canal to link the Forth and the Clyde came from Charles II, in the 17th century. He was very interested in naval and engineering progress but, alas, was usually in debt as well. It's an interesting speculation that had he not poured money into the harbour mole at Tangier, there might just have been monies for a canal across Scotland.

The 35-mile (56km) Forth & Clyde Canal was built to take seagoing craft, avoiding the dangers of sailing north about Scotland, and to facilitate east–west and Atlantic trade. The width of the canal was set at 28ft (8.6m) and the depth at 8ft (2.5m).

Work on the Forth & Clyde Canal began in 1768 by the engineer John Smeaton, architect of the second Eddystone lighthouse. Five years later it had been completed from the Forth to Kirkintilloch, which immediately became a 'port'! Another two years saw the canal reach Maryhill, but then the money once more ran out. In 1777 Glasgow merchants paid to get the branch as far as Hamiltonhill. In 1785, with money raised on the forfeited Jacobite estates, Robert Whitworth, who succeeded Smeaton as engineer, built the then extraordinary Kelvin Aqueduct and took the line to Bowling on the Clyde, a five-year effort. The Glasgow branch was pushed through to Port Dundas, and the short Monkland Canal fed into it.

The 31½-mile (51km) Union Canal was nicknamed 'The Mathematical River', partly because it followed the 240ft (73m) contour with its sinuosities and also because it largely maintained a regular width (35ft/11m) and depth 5ft/1.5m). While we're on figures, in 1834 no fewer than 121,407 passengers travelled the canal. Meals, music, even gaming tables were provided to pass the time, and there was a night sleeper service which was popular with both businessmen and honeymoon couples. Darwin as a student wrote to his sister about going to Glasgow by canal in 1826.

Linlithgow Palace was garrisoned, as the local people were doubtful about the wild Irish navvies on their doorstep. (Two of those people have gained deserved notoriety through a second career: Burke and Hare.) Ironically, much of the expertise gained on building the canals was then used in the construction of the railways that led to the death of the canals. The enormous work done in restoring the canals has provided many ideas and techniques for canal restorations elsewhere. The Falkirk Wheel, a new design of boat lift, was one unique concept and went instantly from inspiration to icon, joined in that status more recently by the dramatic sculpture of the Kelpies.

It is hard to envisage the Scotland of pre-canal times, when the only transport was four-footed, either as riding and pack animals or as haulers of inefficient carts over an almost impossible landscape. With Glasgow and Edinburgh growing, and both domestic and industrial demand for coal reaching a critical stage, there had to be some new development. The Forth & Clyde Canal was a splendid pioneering venture and, not for the first time, the authorities in Edinburgh spent years squabbling over routes and plans

Cruise boats on the Forth & Clyde Canal west of Kilsyth

before agreeing on the Union Canal. (I notice that the Edinburgh provost, who had bitterly opposed the finally accepted plan of Hugh Baird, has his name down among the subscribers.) The original plans were by John Rennie but were superceeded by those of Baird, who had Telford's backing. The sheer scale of the work astonishes. The whole length was divided into lots, and these were allocated to various contractors. It was all pick, shovel and wheelbarrow work, employing thousands of itinerant labourers. The squalor can be imagined. A satellite picture of the time would have shown a dirty brown scar across Scotland. The scar would hardly have healed before the railways were making the canals redundant. Railways had the advantage of being able to go almost anywhere, whereas canals had their linear limitations.

RESTORATION

In 1994 British Waterways announced they would seek funding from the new National Lottery opportunity. That the project finally flew the flag of 'The Millennium Link' hides the years between as hopes rose and fell and many people worked their hearts out on behalf of the dream. Then at last, in 1998, Donald Dewar, Secretary of State for Scotland, announced the funding guarantees, all £78.4 million. This was the minimum needed, and even today millions are still being raised, and spent, as the work of improving and regeneration continues. There were plenty of places with eyesore industrial failures which are now being landscaped or developed tastefully – and that effort is set to continue. How quickly the work settles in never fails to astonish. Do read Guthrie Hutton's book mentioned at the end of this section, for the last chapter tells the saga of restoration and shows pictures of work in progress: a mammoth undertaking. It all looks so natural now, but we must not forget this past. The first edition of his book ended with a promise of great things to come, and we have seen plenty of new initiatives: many more boats active, new stagings and marinas, residential moorings, cafés, restaurants – and the multimillion huge Helix Park with the Kelpies marking the new, improved entry from the River Forth. Scotland has a girdle of gold across her waist.

CYCLISTS AND OTHER TOWPATH USERS

Cycling the canals is popular, but many doing so are commuting or treating the canal as training, and the behaviour of some of these people leaves a lot to be desired, as they disregard cycling codes of conduct and plain good manners. Cyclists *must* warn of their coming when approaching pedestrians from behind; into wind especially they are not heard, and their sudden barging past gives constant shocks, and very real danger, all quite unnecessary. Cycles after all can be bought with a bell attached. Use them! (On one occasion I, quietly walking, was very happy to have sent one miscreant into the canal. He'd stormed up from behind me, unheralded and, as it turned out, just as he was set to pass I moved to the left and shouldered him as a result – and over he went into the water.) I've seen cyclists crash into each other at bridges, get tangled in a dog's long leash, scatter cygnets and cause plenty of general distress. So, cyclists, get your brains in gear.

Many reaches of canal are popular with dog walkers, who are generally well disciplined and cause few problems.

One sorry observation is best made here, rather than as a constant moan through my account of every urban area, and that concerns the litter and graffiti encountered, something on which the authorities are lax and our social conscience fails. The approaches to, and in, Glasgow are far the worst.

The suburbs of both Edinburgh and Glasgow, and through all the milestoning towns along the way, see the heaviest towpath usage, and the jokes about the east–west characteristics are not altogether unfounded. In Edinburgh – out to Ratho, say – about 30% of people met give a greeting; from Broxburn on to the Clyde it's over 70%. Socialising is so rewarding I find; people enjoy a chat, telling of their local area and having their own canal experiences to relate. I can't resist mentioning a personal experience when working on the original guidebook.

I'd stopped to look at Glasgow's Possil Road bridges from below when an urchin, seeing me with clipboard, looking about, asked, "Can ah help ye, meestir?" – and gave me needed information. Soon after I asked a man for directions and he not only gave them but told me of the Bryant and May factory's fine brickwork, which I'd have missed, and pointed out a wee, welcome tearoom. Then, on nearing the canal I was standing in contemplation, wondering whether to head to a bridge, up right, or an overspill, left. There was a group of winos round a fire of pallets on the towpath near the overspill and my hesitation caught the eye of someone of doubtful sobriety who was probably joining them. He cheerfully said, "Dinna mind them, sonny; they'll nae herm ye." A trio of cheery incidents like that just couldn't have happened in Edinburgh. On the other hand, Edinburgh largely avoids Glasgow's sorry vandalism, graffiti and litter.

DEFINITIONS

Some words of canal-speak may need explaining. When areas of canal were filled in, or new bridges broke their line, big drain pipes were laid – *culverts* – to ensure that the actual flow of water continued. The level of water is controlled by having *feeders* and smaller *intakes* to add water, and *overspills* to drain off any excess. By many locks or bridges there are *winding holes*, wide basins where there is room for the long canal boats to turn round. *Stop locks/gates*, usually at bridges, allowed beams to be slotted across the canal to form barriers so a section could be drained for maintenance, etc. (largely abandoned now). On the UC towpath there are rows of stone (getting overgrown) set on the edge of the canal to give horses some purchase when straining to pull barges along; these are *kicking stones*. A *viaduct* is when a 'way' (road, rail, etc.) is carried over water (stream, river, canal) and an

Cyclists at an example of an overspill

*An example of kicking stones
by the Falkirk Tunnel*

aqueduct is where water is carried over any feature. A *bascule bridge* is where a bridge is lifted by a system of counterweights ('bascule' comes from the French word for a seesaw); a *swing bridge* is one that does just that, rotating as against lifting. An *abutment* is the support on which an arch or bridge rests – or indicates where once a bridge existed. Some may have grooves cut in the stonework from the wear of towing ropes. A *compensatory bridge* was one where a bridge had to be made to allow a farmer access to his fields being bisected by the canal. A *change house* was where horses were swopped over so that fresh ones replaced those tiring from their hard labours. (The *Kelpies* are a nod to these noble beasts.) *Residential moorings* are where people may live, rather than stopover, and the prepared sites are easy to spot from allocated colourful quayside huts. A *pend* is a small, short, passageway under some obstruction (like a canal) or through a group of houses (eg The Radical Pend in Castlecary).

Things like these will be pointed out in early chapters, less so later on when, working on the basis that you will follow the route set out in the book, there's the fun of then spotting and recognising them. Many of the new, or rebuilt, bridges have the neat MM on them to commemorate the Millennium restorations.

The necessary, rather odd numbering for new bridges

MAPS

Each chapter heading is followed by the numbers of the Ordnance Survey (OS) maps covering that section. OSLR means Ordnance Survey Landranger, scale 1:50,000, and OSE means Ordnance Survey Explorer 1:25,000. The Landranger covers the canals on Sheets 66, 65, 64. The more detailed Explorer numbers are 350, 349, 348, 342. However, walking the canals with just one map is possible by using the excellent (if slightly dated) special GEO projects/British Waterways map guide *Forth and Clyde and Union Canals (with the Crinan Canal)*. This gives everything one could need: street maps of all towns involved,

An original fare stage marker and milestone

all practical details of the canals themselves, plenty of diagrams and statistics, description of sites – a superb, all-colour, illustrated piece of map-making. Order in any bookshop or from Amazon. (Not being revised or published again when stocks run out.) The maps in this book are only outline sketches and should not be used on their own.

Scottish Canals issue a *Skipper's Guide*, F&CC, UC, which is also full of practical information.

As modern maps are metric I've generally stuck with kilometres and metres, but signposts etc are often in miles and feet (a very British anomaly) and you'll even see cases where distances are metric but give good old vulgar fractions rather than a decimal point (eg 7¾km). Readers will just have to tolerate the variations.

Discover Forth & Clyde: Clyde Routes Map. 1: 10,000. Sustrans. This covers the 66½mls (107km) Edinburgh to Bowling route 754 along the Union and Forth & Clyde Canals.

BOOKS

There are few recent books about the canal. The most important is Hutton, G: *Scotland's Millennium Canals. The Survival and Revival of the Forth*

& Clyde and Union Canals. Stenlake Publishing (2002) which is lavishly illustrated as well as being comprehensive. There is a full bibliography.

Dowds, T J: *The Forth and Clyde Canal, a History*. Tuckwell Press (2003). This is a good narrative, as is the older, well-researched Lindsay: *The Canals of Scotland*. David & Charles (1968) which also has a chapter on the Monkland Canal. Bardwell, S & Megarry, J: *The John Muir Way*. Rucksack Readers (2014), has notes on travel, accommodation etc which is useful.

On some more particular topics, Strathkelvin District Libraries & Museums published several Bowman, AI titles about the *Queens* etc: *Swifts & Queens* (1984), *The Gipsy o' Kirky* (1987), *Kirkintilloch Shipbuilding* (1983). They also published Martin, D & Maclean, A: *Edinburgh & Glasgow Railway Guidebook* (1992). Most can be found in the Kirkintilloch Library. Haldane, A R B, *The Drove Roads of Scotland* is a classic still in print. Hanson, W H and Maxwell, G S: *Rome's North-West Frontier – The Antonine Wall,* EUP (1983) is useful, and Brown, H M: *A Scottish Gravestones Miscellany,* Birlinn (2008) covers that topic. Scott, A's *The Kelpies* 2014, is a sumptuous book on this icon.

Matheson, A: *Glasgow's Other River: Exploring the Kelvin* (2000) ranges widely over both the rural section of the river and as it runs through Glasgow. Most of the big towns, like Linlithgow, Falkirk, Kilsyth, Kirkintilloch, have specific histories, mostly long out of print, but available in their libraries which always have heritage sections. LUCS and Kirkintilloch Library have some publications on sale. LUCS have reproduced the inexpensive booklet *Companion for Canal Passengers betwixt Edinburgh and Glasgow* (1823) which is fun to read.

The iconic mural on Lothian House in Edinburgh

Maps

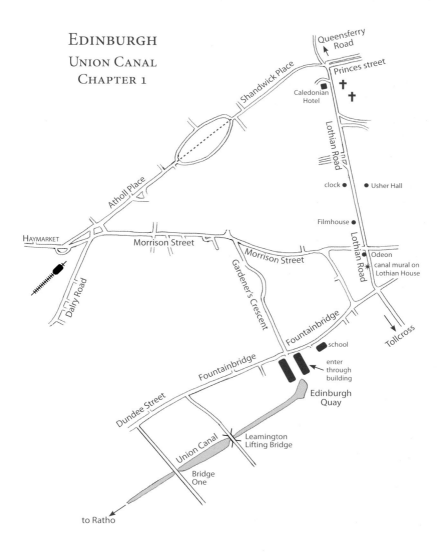

EDINBURGH
UNION CANAL
CHAPTER 1

Queensferry Road

Princes street

Shandwick Place

Caledonian Hotel

Lothian Road

clock ● ● Usher Hall

Filmhouse ●

Atholl Place

Lothian Road

Odeon
canal mural on
Lothian House

HAYMARKET

Morrison Street

Morrison Street

Dalry Road

Gardener's Crescent

Fountainbridge

Tollcross

school

enter
through
building

Fountainbridge

Edinburgh
Quay

Dundee Street

Union Canal

Leamington
Lifting Bridge

Bridge
One

to Ratho

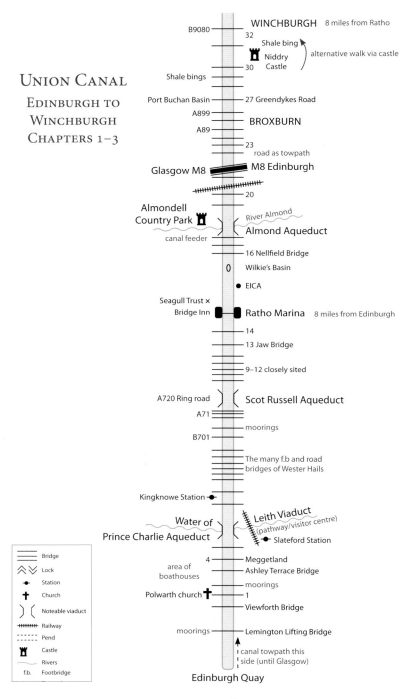

UNION CANAL

EDINBURGH TO WINCHBURGH

CHAPTERS 1–3

WINCHBURGH   8 miles from Ratho

B9080 — 32

Shale bing

Niddry Castle   } alternative walk via castle

30

Shale bings

Port Buchan Basin — 27 Greendykes Road

A899

A89

BROXBURN

23

road as towpath

Glasgow M8   M8 Edinburgh

20

Almondell Country Park

River Almond

Almond Aqueduct

canal feeder

16 Nellfield Bridge

0   Wilkie's Basin

EICA

Seagull Trust ✕
Bridge Inn   Ratho Marina   8 miles from Edinburgh

14

13 Jaw Bridge

9–12 closely sited

A720 Ring road   Scot Russell Aqueduct

A71

moorings

B701

The many f.b and road bridges of Wester Hails

Kingknowe Station

Water of   Leith Viaduct
(pathway/visitor centre)

Prince Charlie Aqueduct

Slateford Station

4   Meggetland

area of boathouses   Ashley Terrace Bridge

moorings

Polwarth church   1

Viewforth Bridge

moorings   Lemington Lifting Bridge

canal towpath this side (until Glasgow)

Edinburgh Quay

Bridge
Lock
Station
Church
Noteable viaduct
Railway
Pend
Castle
Rivers
f.b.   Footbridge

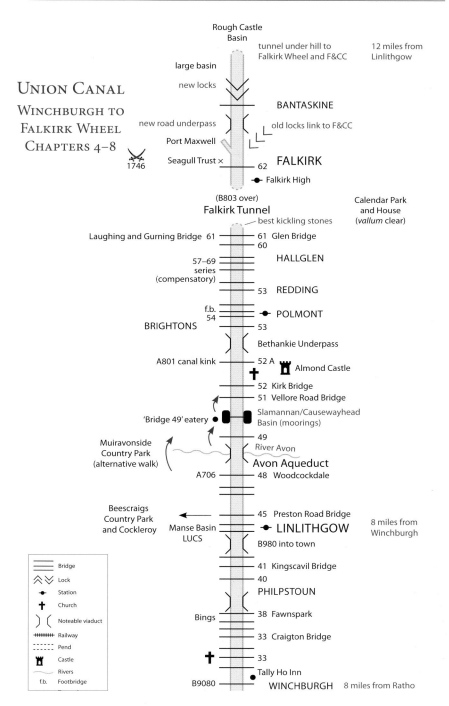

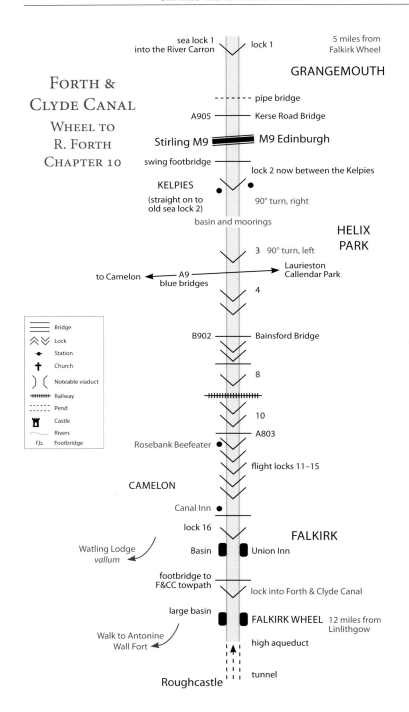

FORTH & CLYDE CANAL

WHEEL TO R. FORTH

CHAPTER 10

sea lock 1 into the River Carron

lock 1

5 miles from Falkirk Wheel

GRANGEMOUTH

pipe bridge

A905 — Kerse Road Bridge

Stirling M9 ▬▬▬ M9 Edinburgh

swing footbridge

lock 2 now between the Kelpies

KELPIES
(straight on to old sea lock 2)

90° turn, right

basin and moorings

HELIX PARK

3   90° turn, left

to Camelon ← A9 blue bridges → Laurieston Callendar Park

4

B902 — Bainsford Bridge

8

10

A803

Rosebank Beefeater

flight locks 11–15

CAMELON

Canal Inn

lock 16

FALKIRK

Watling Lodge *vallum*

Basin   Union Inn

footbridge to F&CC towpath

lock into Forth & Clyde Canal

large basin

FALKIRK WHEEL   12 miles from Linlithgow

Walk to Antonine Wall Fort

high aqueduct

tunnel

Roughcastle

Legend:
- ═══ Bridge
- ⋀ ⋁ Lock
- •─ Station
- ✝ Church
-) (Noteable viaduct
- ┼┼┼┼┼ Railway
- ----- Pend
- ♜ Castle
- ～ Rivers
- f.b. Footbridge

FORTH &
CLYDE CANAL
WHEEL TO
WYNDFORD LOCK
CHAPTERS 11, 12

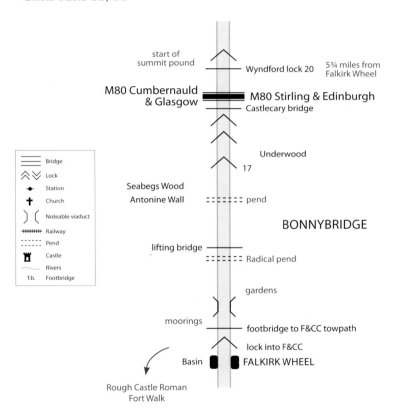

start of
summit pound

Wyndford lock 20   5¾ miles from
                      Falkirk Wheel

M80 Cumbernauld
& Glasgow   M80 Stirling & Edinburgh
                     Castlecary bridge

Underwood
17

Seabegs Wood
Antonine Wall   pend

BONNYBRIDGE

lifting bridge
                     Radical pend

gardens

moorings
                     footbridge to F&CC towpath

                     lock into F&CC

Basin   FALKIRK WHEEL

Rough Castle Roman
Fort Walk

Legend:
Bridge
Lock
Station
Church
Noteable viaduct
Railway
Pend
Castle
Rivers
f.b.   Footbridge

FORTH & CLYDE CANAL

WYNDFORD LOCK –
AUCHINSTARRY – TWECHAR
Roman Wall, Kilsyth

CHAPTERS 12–15

Legend:
	Bridge
≫	Lock
	Station
✝	Church
)(	Noteable viaduct
▦▦▦▦	Railway
▥▥▥▥	Pend
)(	Rivers
f.b.	Footbridge
	Towpath
	Built up areas

N

to M80

to M80 and Cumbernauld

Lock 20
P
Wyndford
6 miles to Twechar

A803

KELVINHEAD

BANTON

A803

Dullatur Bog
(SSS1)

Banton Resevoir

✕ 1645

stable ruin

feeder

Old Craigmarloch
Basin

to Dullatur & Cumbernauld

KILSYTH HILLS

Colzium House

Burngreen

Walkway

KILSYTH

quarry

Coach Road

AUCHINSTARRY

Boathouse

Croy Hill

quarry

quarry

P

mausoleum
graveyard

A803

to Milton of
Campsie
Kirkintilloch

to A803

B8023

lifting
bridge

Shirva

pend

Twechar
6 miles
from
Wyndford
Lock

Bar
Hill

155m

Castle
Hill

▲

Roman
site

B8002

to Croy
Station

to Cumbernauld

to M80

to Kirkintilloch

xxvi

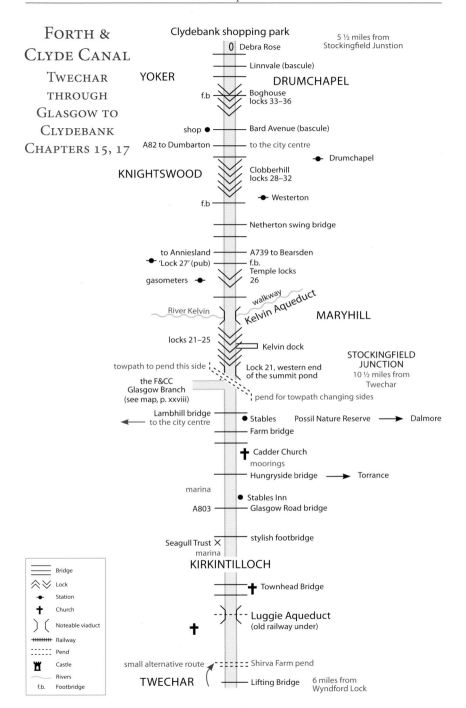

FORTH &
CLYDE CANAL

TWECHAR
THROUGH
GLASGOW TO
CLYDEBANK
CHAPTERS 15, 17

Clydebank shopping park

5 ½ miles from
Stockingfield Junstion

0 Debra Rose

Linnvale (bascule)

YOKER

DRUMCHAPEL

f.b
Boghouse
locks 33–36

shop ●
Bard Avenue (bascule)

A82 to Dumbarton
to the city centre

●─ Drumchapel

KNIGHTSWOOD
Clobberhill
locks 28–32

f.b
─●─ Westerton

Netherton swing bridge

to Anniesland
A739 to Bearsden
●─ 'Lock 27' (pub)
f.b.
Temple locks
gasometers ─●
26

walkway

Kelvin Aqueduct

River Kelvin
MARYHILL

locks 21–25
Kelvin dock
STOCKINGFIELD
JUNCTION
10 ½ miles from
Twechar

towpath to pend this side
Lock 21, western end
of the summit pond

the F&CC
Glasgow Branch
(see map, p. xxviii)
pend for towpath changing sides

Lambhill bridge
● Stables
Possil Nature Reserve ──→ Dalmore
to the city centre

Farm bridge

✝ Cadder Church
moorings

Hungryside bridge ──→ Torrance

marina
● Stables Inn

A803
Glasgow Road bridge

Seagull Trust ✕
stylish footbridge
marina

KIRKINTILLOCH

✝ Townhead Bridge

)─(Luggie Aqueduct
(old railway under)

✝

small alternative route
Shirva Farm pend

TWECHAR (
Lifting Bridge
6 miles from
Wyndford Lock

═══	Bridge
⩘⩗	Lock
─•─	Station
✝	Church
) (	Noteable viaduct
┼┼┼┼┼┼	Railway
┄┄┄	Pend
♜	Castle
⌇	Rivers
f.b	Footbridge

The Glasgow Branch
Forth & Clyde Canal

only important features shown

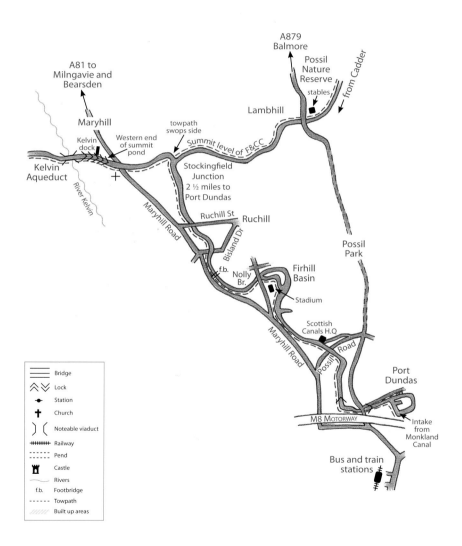

Legend:

Bridge
Lock
Station
Church
Noteable viaduct
Railway
Pend
Castle
Rivers
f.b.	Footbridge
Towpath
Built up areas

Forth & Clyde Canal
Clydebank to Bowling
Chapter 17

Bowling Station

Clyde Sealock

4 miles from
Clydebank
Shopping Park

marina

Old Custom House

onetime Caledonian railway bridge

(bascule)

marina

OLD KILPATRICK

Ferrydyke (bascule)

ERSKINE BRIDGE

A898

lock 37

Saltings Nature
Reserve

Erskine Ferry Bridge (swing)

Farm Road (bascule)

Dalmuir

A814 to Dumbarton

A814 to Glasgow

Dalmuir Drop lock

f.b.

CLYDEBANK

Singer Station

A8014

CLYDEBANK SHOPPING PARK

5½ miles from
Stockingfield
Junction

Sylvania Way footbridges

0 *Debra Rose*

═══	Bridge
⋀ ⋁	Lock
●	Station
✝	Church
) (	Noteable viaduct
⊞⊞⊞⊞	Railway
------	Pend
♜	Castle
∿	Rivers
f.b.	Footbridge

The Union Canal

1

Edinburgh to the Almond Aqueduct
OSLR 66, 65; OSE 350

Lothian House on Lothian Road, a five-minute walk from the west end of Princes Street in the heart of Edinburgh, has a mural depicting a horse-drawn canal barge on the Union Canal and the wording 'Here Stood Port Hopetoun'. To me this has always been the poignant symbol of times past, but walk on another five minutes and the present canal terminus, Edinburgh Quay, is reached. This is just one of the latest developments following the rebirth of the canals across Scotland, a landmark for times to come.

Lothian House was built in 1922 on the site of the basin named after the Earl of Hopetoun, a major early investor whose collieries supplied much of Edinburgh's coal. Off at a tangent near the end (reaching to Morrison Street) lay the coaling basin of Port Hamilton, another name that nods to a grandee investor. Another basin, Lochrin Basin, lay south of Fountainbridge and served the brewery – at the time of writing demolished and developments underway. The basin had closed, even before Port Hopetoun and Port Hamilton were filled in and 'developed' in the 1920s. By then the whole area had become seedy and neglected. A new basin, just the stump of the amputated original, was then called Lochrin Basin.

With the Millennium Link project restoring navigation coast to coast and city to city (the Forth & Clyde Canal completed in 2001 and the Falkirk Wheel/Union Canal in 2002) ambitious plans were made for revitalising both the Edinburgh and Glasgow city centre termini of the canals.

Walking down Lothian Road, keep on the east side to best see the canal mural on Lothian House, very much a Twenties building with a touch of art deco, then, next right, head along Fountainbridge. Hard to think this area was once the site of busy canal basins. One survival is a pair of arches to the then Edinburgh Meat Market, dated 1884. Pass Tollcross Primary School and before the roundabout cut through, left, and you are on Edinburgh Quay, the city end of the Union Canal today. If coming from Haymarket Station, head up Morrison Street then right along Gardner's Crescent to reach this roundabout and Edinburgh Quay. Edinburgh Quay is well hidden among the big modern edifices which give this area of the city its architectural flavour.

This rump of water was once the scene of a headline-grabbing accident. George Meikle Kemp, the creator of the Scott Monument, was a shy, rather odd character whose design was only chosen because of an impasse in awarding the contract. He was the compromise candidate. He was more joiner than architect, and his design incorporated ideas ranging from Melrose Abbey to Rouen Cathedral, but then Scott himself was constantly stealing ideas if not actual structures as he built Abbotsford, his dream house near Melrose.

Kemp had been to see his contractor (the stone presumably being delivered via the Union Canal) and left to walk home along the towpath on a cold, dark, foggy night. A week later the first evidence of a tragedy was when his stick and hat floated to the surface. He is buried in St Cuthbert's, the church down in the dell below the meeting of Princes Street and Lothian Road. Others buried there include artist Alexander Nasmyth (whose bridge you will see on the River Almond) and the drug-using writer Thomas de Quincy.

The Leamington lifting bridge and the Edinburgh end of the Union Canal

Viewforth Bridge in Edinburgh with the symbol for Glasgow above the western keystone

The first stretch of canal (Union Path) is overlooked by flats, restaurants, offices and other developments (more to come on the demolished brewery site) and there's even a 'boatel' beside the welcoming flock of sculpted swans – their heads shiny from patting hands. The south side of the canal along to and beyond the lifting bridge provides moorings, occupied by colourful resident canal boats. The 1896 Leamington Lifting Bridge originally stood near Port Hamilton. Still operational, its hydraulics are powered by electricity. The whole canal combination through to the Clyde is the Sustrans Route 754, and cycling coast to coast is proving ever more popular.

The towpath is on the north bank of the wandering Union Canal, and throughout the bridges are numbered on the keystones, 1 to 62, although some bridges have been replaced and new ones have been given numbers like 6A, 6B and so on. The first bridge we come to, Viewforth Bridge, has a carving of a symbolic castle over the keystone on the Edinburgh side and Glasgow's fish and tree over the western keystone. There are several utilitarian iron bridges (without numbers) before Bridge 4 (Meggetland Bridge) is reached and the numbering takes on its real interest. Sadly, there's a plethora of graffiti on bridges and walls.

This first mile often has swans, ducks, coots and moorhens that seem oblivious to human activity, unless rushing for bread thrown by residents of the modern flats overlooking the canal on the south bank and big developments on the towpath side. A bridge is passed (no access) and then older tenements overlook the jungly canal.

The canal curves, and the green sweep of Harrison Park appears on the right. The next colourfully painted iron bridge (Harrison Road) has the massive red sandstone Polwarth Parish Church beside it, and beyond lies the Forth Canoe Club boathouse and a variety of hiring and cruising craft including the cruise restaurant longboat *Zazou*. The Ogilvie Terrace Moorings has a launching slip, winding hole and all the facilities for cruising: water, electric hook-up, rubbish disposal etc. There are rowing boats for hire at weekends. The wide iron bridge, with spiky finials, carries Ashley Terrace. Continuing, the houses stand back from the banks and the feeling is more rural.

The Edinburgh University boathouses lie on the far bank, and this stretch has several club houses and stages for launching, with the chance of watching the strenuous exercise. There are boathouses and stagings before and after the Meggetland pair of bridges, the first a modern concrete horizontal structure, the second an example of the original standard

Union Canal bridges' style: inscribed 'Bridge 4'. Housing lines the canal's banks. There's a battered old milestone, then a metal footbridge/pipeline combination linking Allan Park Road on the north and Craiglockhart on the south.

The canal wiggles along its contour to reach the next landmark, the high Prince Charlie Aqueduct, which was rebuilt in 1937, one of the better concrete bridges of that vintage when seen from Slateford Road, which it spans. The name perhaps comes from the Pretender setting up camp close by in 1745 to await the surrender of the city. A flight of steps leads down for shops or bus. There are then stagings, mooring rings and kicking stones. Soon comes 'one of the finest works of its kind' (*Companion*), the eight-arched Slateford Aqueduct, 152m (500ft) long and 23m (75)ft above the Water of Leith, with the canal carried in an iron trough. This fine aqueduct, Scotland's second largest, is now rather hemmed in by the busy Slateford Road to the south, and a lower, but fine, arched railway bridge to the north. There is an overspill at the east end of the aqueduct, the overflow spraying down into the Water of Leith. Hugh Baird is the engineer responsible for the Union's trio of great aqueducts, this one marginally bigger than the Almond Aqueduct.

On the Union Canal,
Meggetland, Edinburgh

From the Slateford Aqueduct to the rail viaduct spanning the Water of Leith walkway

Just before the aqueduct a flight of 86 steps descends to reach a sturdy footwalk passing under the aqueduct and railway viaduct – part of the Water of Leith Walkway. Left lies the fascinating Water of Leith Centre with information and interpretive displays, coffee bar, and the first public toilet since leaving Edinburgh Quay. The Water of Leith rises in the Pentlands and can be followed afoot (or cycled) right through the city to the sea.

A stump of milestone and staging marks the west end of the aqueduct, and the towpath runs parallel with the A70 Lanark road to an iron girder of a bridge with the far abutment strapped up. There's a signpost and a sculpted indicator for the National Cycle Network (75) and a sign for the Millennium Acres Community Woodland, then the first of several tree sculptures: of two men, one with a spade, the other holding a rock, carved from a tree in situ. Railings mark a low, arched, abandoned underpass, then the railway angles across the canal. Bridge 5 is in standard MM style, then playing fields are passed (Hailes Quarry Park). The park was once a quarry 100ft (30m) deep. Much of the stone went to London. Huge tower blocks now dominate the south shore.

The canal was culverted for about a mile through this big housing development, so cutting it again was another major undertaking, carried out with the usual flair of the Millennium Link restorations. The new crossings that were needed have played havoc with the numbering of the bridges. The next, after an overspill, is 5AA, and is twinned with an older bridge which does not have a number. To work past the dominating, quite stylish tower blocks, we have Bridges 6, 6A, a black horizontal footbridge, and 6B (all in MM form). Beside another tree sculpture seat, of a frog, there's a long section of moorings. Bridge piles on bridge again: a high arched footbridge, another horizontal black one, and Bridge 6C, beside which is a dock with a dragon sculpture (south bank). Residential moorings (and winding hole) are unused (no security from vandalism). Bridge 7 follows (milestone 4/27½) then, with ever-increasing traffic roar, there's a last black footbridge and an overspill.

Wester Hailes

The canal re-emerged here during the years of culverting, and now swings right – the Murray Burn goes under – to reach Calder Quay/Bridge 8 Hub and the last tree sculpture, of otters and swans this time. A concrete flyover (the A71 Livingston/Kilmarnock road) replaces its close neighbour, an original Bridge 8, then there's a MM Bridge 8A and the canal swings left to reach the Scott Russell Aqueduct which crosses 170ft (56m) over the ring road, a noisy fascination, continuing awhile as the 1995 M8/M9 link sweeps parallel to the winding canal. A milestone before the aqueduct neatly indicates 5 miles back the way – and 26½ to go. The aqueduct was constructed in 1987.

Scott Russell (d.1882) was an engineer and naval architect who discovered what was called the Solitary Wave Theory on the canal here. When his craft stopped he noticed a wave went on ahead, unchanged, a long way. This fascinated him and led to the wave-line principle of ship construction – and, in the 1960s, to application with fibre optics.

The Scott Russell Aqueduct over the city's ring road

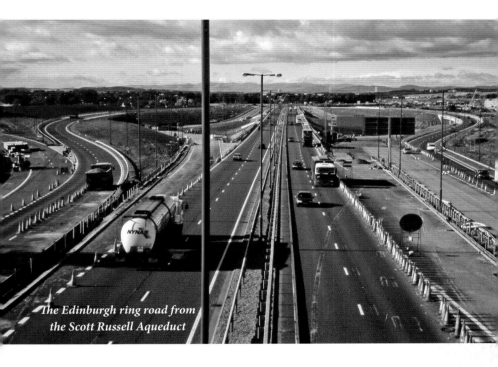

The Edinburgh ring road from the Scott Russell Aqueduct

Bridges 9 and 10 soon follow, now cut off from traffic, the latter with a launching spot on the south side (where I once came on a dozy cormorant), then Gogar Station Road Bridge 10A, built pre-millennium (1995) with stone abutments and a shapely concrete arch with white railings. Bridges 11 and 12 soon follow, the latter taking a small road north over the M8. Bridge 13, Jaw Bridge, as many, has a winding hole.

At the start of Ratho there's a graceful iron seat with a panel showing canal wildlife, then a small perching seat which commemorates the nearby stage marker with a notice '1832. To Edinburgh 7 miles, fare 6d [2.5p], To Falkirk 25 miles, fare 1/6 [7.5p]'. Another old milestone stands beside the stage post for stages one and two (hard to decipher). Across the canal and on to Bridge 15 in Ratho is a long reach of residential moorings, well used. There are one or two more attractive resting seats (which continue beyond Bridge 15). There's a big turning area and a swing footbridge over the towpath leading to a marina, and then a picnic area with a superb sculpture of a horse-drawn barge in the old days (see page 129).

In its heyday, Ratho had 14 pubs. The Pop Inn, next to the canal, is reputed to have had a door at each end of the building so the bargeman in charge of the towing horse could enter by one door, enjoy a pint *en passant*, and exit by the other door without having fallen behind his charge. In about 1845 Ratho House was turned into a distillery, the annual production of 42,000 gallons being largely consumed locally. Canal work was obviously a drouthy business.

One of Edinburgh's regular exports via the canal was manure (horses rather than horsepower in those days) and this led to great fertility on the canalside farms. Maybe this lingers on, as two local farms hold world records for wheat production. Coal (and building stone) was the big import to the city, and the major reason for the canal being built. The passenger side was never lucrative and was soon killed off by the railways.

The Bridge Inn was originally a farm, then a staging post on the canal, now it is renowned for the excellence of its food, the friendly service and delightful setting. It is also the base of the Edinburgh Canal Centre, which offers a variety of cruises with the two restaurant canal boats, the *Pride of the Union* and *Pride of Belhaven*. These often go along to the Almond Aqueduct where people dine on board ('in the air' it feels) or al fresco on the bank. In the festive season, there are even cruises to Santa's Secret Island – once seen on Blue Peter.

The Seagull Trust is also based here, and runs trips for disabled passengers in the *Mackay Seagull*, *Edinburgh Crusader* and *St John Crusader II*. Their first cruise took place in 1979; now over 5,000 people are involved annually, and there are other boats based at Falkirk, Kirkintilloch and Inverness.

Ratho is a neat little village and, before continuing, do have a look at the old cemetery round the church over the bridge on the north side of Ratho (Baird Road commemorates the canal's engineer). The church lies behind the war memorial. Left of the door is an unusual gravestone shaped like a coffin; on its side the inscription indicates the incumbent suffered 'an instantaneous death from a stroke by a thrashing (*sic*) machine' (early 19th century).

Ratho is a major canal access point and has several car parks. From the Newbridge roundabout turn off for Newbridge, then, almost at once left, and follow Edinburgh Canal Centre/Ratho signs. Leaving Edinburgh by the A71, the turning off by Dalmahoy Road is similarly signposted.

Back on the canal from Bridge 15, you pass the old change house, an area for visitor moorings (with clear kicking stones) before the Ratho Hall grounds (walled garden). A peaceful, deep-set, woody section with mature

Ratho

trees follows, shading both banks. A staging beside steps up indicates the Edinburgh International Climbing Arena, where a five-storey-high quarry has been roofed over to create the largest indoor rock-climbing facility in the world. A spectacle not to be missed. (Spectator gallery/café.) The next high bridge over the canal is the road in to the EICA. The arena is signposted from the hectic Newbridge roundabout. From the A71 out of Edinburgh turn onto the B7030 at Wilkieston, continue through Bonnington and on to the entrance (right). From Ratho take the road for Bonnington and turn right onto the B7030. There's one of the best examples of kicking stones along this deeply wooded reach.

In the Edinburgh International Climbing Arena

Once out of the trees there is quite a contrast, for the M8 swings alongside the canal for a while to share its roar and bustle. There is a wider section, Wilkie's Basin, with an island in it (Santa's Island in season for Ratho cruises), then you cross the B7030 road (Bonnington Aqueduct) from Newbridge to Wilkieston, on an aqueduct which was reconstructed in 1978. Timbers dredged up in the basin are thought to be from one of the 'Swifts' which carried passengers from Edinburgh to Falkirk in three and a half hours. Pulled by two horses (changed periodically) they had prior right of way and charged along in style. The M8 has small tunnels under it for the use of wildlife.

After a spell without bridges, numbers 16, 17 and 18 come in quick succession. By the attractive setting of Bridge 16, Nellfield Bridge, you may spot the narrowboat *Thomas Telford*, normally moored in that idyllic spot. Bridge 17 is a fine high arch with Clifton Hall School to the north, Bridge 18 has a rustic feel (with railings), then, quite dramatically, you reach the high Almond Aqueduct. There is little warning: you round a bend and are on it. On the other side there is a basin, wharf and car park, with the major feeder for the canal alongside. Upstream lies Almondell (and Calderwood) Country Park, which is well worth a diversionary visit and will be described in the next section.

The car park opposite can be reached from Newbridge, taking the B7030 which passes under the railway, M8 and the Bonnington Aqueduct. Follow 'Union Canal' signs thereafter. There is access onto the aqueduct's towpath side – long flights of steps down and up link the two sides. On the wall by the towpath is the date 1821. The drive passing under the canal is private, going to Lin's Mill. There is no mill now, but Lin's Grave is hidden away in the woods of the grounds and is inscribed 'Here lyeth the dust of William Lin richt heritor of Lins Miln who died in the year of the Lord 1645'. He was one of the many victims of the plague which ravished Scotland that year.

The boats cruising from Ratho often turn at this spot after sailing out onto the great aqueduct. Those cruising may enjoy a buffet supper ashore, and I saw one wedding charter thoroughly enjoying life. An 1834 handbill, offering ten-mile (16km) trips for sixpence (equivalent to about £15 in the early 2000s) noted that here, "fruits, confectioneries and varieties of refreshment can be had". Now, sadly, litter louts just leave their chip supper debris behind.

2

Almondell Country Park
OSLR 65; OSE 350

This attractive park has the main Union Canal feeder running down through it, so is of particular interest for those walking the canal. The feeder outlet is visible on the south side of the canal beside the staging and winding hole, immediately before the Almond Aqueduct, but to reach it means negotiating a set of steps down and up again under the aqueduct.

Walk out from the canalside car park, and after about 250m there are steps (signposted, right, for Almondell Country Park) which drop down to the feeder aqueduct, here going into a final tunnel to reach the canal basin. Turn left and walk up the glen. Across the way Illieston Castle stands boldly against the skyline, and downstream, as one progresses, is seen the canal aqueduct, a splendid, buttressed structure. Illieston Castle is a well-preserved tower house, built by John Ellis in 1665 but with earlier buildings going back much further. James II and James IV both used it as a hunting lodge.

The path along by the feeder is clear, so needs little detailing. There are plenty of gates and stiles and interest in seeing how streams are led under the feeder. Neat compensatory bridges bring farm tracks down to riverside fields and periodically the feeder vanishes into conduits, tunnels cut because of spurs in the wending glen. At one spot the river runs hard against the flank so the path heads up, only to descend again by steps. Shortly after, the attractive houses of Shiel Mill lie below and the tarred road into them is crossed.

Where the feeder comes out of another tunnel a steep path goes up, left (Larchwood Walk), but drops down to the graceful single tower suspension bridge across the River Almond. It was built by the Royal Engineers in 1970 and received a Civic Trust Award. In 1986 it was named the Mandela Bridge. Bright laburnums in season, and big chestnut trees.

Cross the grassy picnic and play area, once the old walled garden of Almondell House, to reach the park's Visitor Centre buildings, housed in the stable block of the former mansion. This had a connection with the 18th-century Erskine family. The 11th Earl of Buchan lived at nearby Kirkhill House, and a brother, Henry, built the Almondell mansion. The earl died with no issue to inherit, so much of the Kirkhill contents came to Almondell, and Henry's son inherited the title in 1829. (Another brother, Thomas Erskine, was a famed forensic lawyer.) Henry Erskine himself was also a famous lawyer – he twice became Lord Advocate. He started building Almondell in 1790 to his own eccentric design. It was a disastrous enterprise, but he loved the setting which we enjoy today, although we have the additional benefit of the trees in their splendid maturity. The house was damaged by fire in the 1950s and demolished by the army in 1969. Its site, which you pass later, is marked by a parking place for disabled drivers.

Mathematician, astronomer, antiquarian and scholar, the Earl of Buchan constructed a scale model of the solar system in and around the grounds of Kirkhill House in 1776. The model consisted of the Sun, Mercury, Venus, the Earth and its moon, Mars, Jupiter and its four moons, and Saturn with its rings and five moons. Mars is now known to have two moons, Jupiter eleven moons and Saturn nine, and since the construction of the model the planets Neptune, Uranus, Pluto and more bodies have been discovered. Even bearing this in mind, the model was extraordinarily accurate. It was constructed to a scale of 12,238.28 miles to an inch (approximately 1:775 million), the Sun being represented by a stone sphere six feet in diameter, and the Earth by a bronze sphere 0.646 inches in diameter placed 645 feet (196m) away. The larger planets were made, like the Sun, of stone, while the smaller planets were of bronze.

The model has disappeared, but a summary of the calculations which enabled the Earl to construct the model are preserved on a stone pillar which Buchan originally erected in the grounds of Kirkhill in 1777. Buchan also included on the pillar a prediction of the position of the planets on 20 May 2255. Why he chose this date is not known. The pillar was surmounted by a bell tower, on top of which was a metal cross. After Buchan's death, the bell tower was removed and taken to his younger brother's estate at Almondell, where it was placed in front of the stables over a well (which is still there). The pillar remained at Kirkhill, but by the late 1970s it had collapsed. When the shell of Kirkhill House was sold for private restoration, the stones of the pillar were taken into safekeeping by the West Lothian History and Amenity Society, and it was decided to rebuild the pillar, with bell tower and cross, in front of the Visitor Centre at Almondell. And there it is today.

The Visitor Centre (opened in 1981) is a lively, friendly place with interesting historical and wildlife displays, and an attractive small aquarium. It is the base for the park ranger service. Soft drinks, tea, snacks, etc are on sale if you need refreshments – with garden benches outside and a snug conservatory within.

Walk on up the drive through the disabled car park. There are some fine specimen trees, including chestnut, copper beech, cypress, red cedar and sequoia, but most eye-catching are the lime trees with great bunches of suckering growths round their bases – good shelter for wintering birds! Most garden birds will be seen, and perhaps wren, tree creeper, woodpecker, robin, wagtail, dipper and mallard, with goosander, cormorant and herons fishing in the river, on occasion a kingfisher. Bats, roe deer, fox, badger, squirrel, rabbit and even otter have been noted. The small Dell Bridge on the drive was built in 1784 by Henry Erskine, his first piece of landscaping here.

Then there's a large, ornate, double-arched bridge across the River Almond which was designed by the portrait painter and garden landscaper Alexander Naismith and built about 1800. Nasmythe (there are other spellings as well) is best remembered for his iconic portrait of his friend Rabbie Burns, thought to be the only authentic likeness of the poet. The bridge was restored in 1997–8, as it had partly collapsed in 1973 because of burst internal pipes.

Have a look but don't cross the bridge – continue up the west bank of the Almond. Further on, at a weir, you may wonder about a pulley system across the river to a small building. It is a SEPA (Scottish Environmental Protection Agency) gauging station where regular information is collected and river quality monitored. Once a month samples are taken from the river, usually by just wading out – but in a spate the samples can be collected by using a gondola along the wire!

Continuing, the path comes to the green arched ironwork of an unusual bridge – it carries the canal feeder (remember the feeder?) across the River Almond, and has a walkway on top of that; I heard an excited child say, "Look! I'm walking on water". It dates to 1820, part of Hugh Baird's canal work.

Still keeping to the west bank, the next structure over feeder and river is the high (23m/75ft), nine-arched 1885 Camps Viaduct, which once led to mines, brickworks and oil industry sites at Pumpherston and Uphall. The roofed structure below it, like an extended church gateway, is thought to have been built as a precaution against anything being dropped off the viaduct.

A pedestrian bridge and feeder bridge combined to cross the River Almond

Further on, the instruments in the feeder and a sluice gate at a footbridge are more SEPA recording/control works. Continuing, the East Calder Sewage Works are seen, built in 1960 on the creation of Livingston New Town which lies to the west of this rural world, a sprawl of 40,000 inhabitants now (hence the SEPA sites). On a bit, take the bridge (signposted as a cycle way) across the feeder and gain the sturdy footbridge (Pipe Bridge, 1960) which spans the Almond. This is the end of our exploration for, just upstream from the bridge, we see the sluice and weir across the river which creates the start of the canal feeder. As many as two million gallons a day may be added to the canal. The river starts away to the west near Harthill (the well-known watershed when motoring the M8) and eventually flows into the Forth at Cramond. A reservoir, Cobbinshaw (the *Companion* has Barbauchly), was built in the Pentlands to provide extra water, which flows down the Bog Burn, joins the Muirieston Water, then Linhouse Water before meeting the Almond. The aqueduct crosses 22m (70ft) above the River Almond – hence the length of the feeder. It seldom flows faster than 2mph. The feeder channel here is full of monkey flower, bittersweet, greater willowherb (an aquatic cousin of the rosebay species which is also plentiful) and blue water mint.

The Calderwood Country Park lies as a continuation upstream, but is perhaps best left for a visit when the canal does not claim all our attention. It is the largest surviving old woodland in West Lothian, and an SSSI.

Head back down the feeder, but at the small SEPA bridge, it is well worthwhile to cross it and climb up to the airy viaduct for the good views. Down again, continue to the unique bridge taking both feeder and pedestrians over the Almond – a rather odd experience. Cross. Walk down across a meadow to the Nasmythe Bridge. Two alternatives:

1. From the feeder end of the bridge, head off up on a rough path to join the Larchwood Walk, a wide avenue high on the east side of the Almond. It ends with steep steps zigzagging down to near the Mandela Bridge. The Visitor Centre is a few minutes away if refreshments are wanted. Or

2. Cross the Nasmythe Bridge and follow a riverside path back to the Centre. The Dell Bridge looks attractive in passing.

It only remains to wander back down the feeder path to the canal basin by the great aqueduct, completing a visit of many interests beside the canal technicalities.

3

Almond Aqueduct to Winchburgh
OSLR 65; OSE 350

The Almond Aqueduct, the UC's third largest, is impressively high and exposed, with the narrow, cobbled pathway edging the iron trough of the canal. On the right, an airy iron railing does little to hide the 70ft (22m) drop to the River Almond. In spate, the flat island downstream can be covered with water. The aqueduct is 420ft (128m) in length. There is a superb view north, down the river, to Telford's Almond Valley Viaduct on the main Edinburgh–Glasgow Railway. This was built in 1842 and, with 36 arches, somewhat surpasses the aqueduct's mere five. The viaduct contains over a million cubic feet of masonry. Never intended for today's weights and speeds, it has suffered somewhat and is strapped up to support the big arches; an impressive sight. The control sluice, in the middle of the south side of the aqueduct, tends to dribble water, and in severe winters this overflow has been known to freeze solid, creating a remarkable pillar of ice, as in a two-month spell in 1895, recorded in the photograph. At

1895

*On the Almond Aqueduct
(overspill on right)*

the west end of the aqueduct there is a milestone marked 10 (to Edinburgh) and 21 (to Falkirk). About 100m further on an overflow channel, lined with granite setts, crosses the towpath. Bridge 19 (Broomflats Bridge) is just for a farm track, but the minor road bridge, 20, starts a more interesting stretch, with a railway bridge ahead. There's a signpost with distances to everywhere. Probably most satisfying is Edinburgh 12. The railway is the Edinburgh–Uphall–Bathgate–Coatbridge–Glasgow line, which breaks off from the main Edinburgh–Glasgow line north-west of Ratho (Newbridge Junction), and was originally built in 1849 to Bathgate, being extended to Airdrie and Glasgow in 1879. It served the coal, iron and shale oil industries, and the last passenger train was in 1956. The creation of Livingston New Town failed to provide new passengers, and the line west to Airdrie was lifted in 1982. Bathgate station was gutted by an arsonist. Out of this dismal history came resurrection, and the line to Bathgate, an unusual modern station, is now a busy commuter route. The railway bridge (not numbered) is, like quite a few of them, home to nesting swallows each summer. Squeezed between railway and M8, Bridge 21 (Kilpunt Bridge) just gives rural access, then we face the frantic motorway. When the canal was built there was no M8, of course, and its development caused a major blockage and set a problem for any reinstating of the canal – so the M8 was slightly raised, and by making an S bend the canal passes under the motorway. (You can work out where the original line ran.)Bridge 22 just serves Learielaw Farm, a nice name. (Others hereabouts include Loup-o-Lees, Birdsmill, Pumpherston, Powflats and Lookaboutye.) The next Bridge, 23, Drumshoreland Bridge, has a cluster of buildings, and is a Scottish Canals visitor mooring site with all the facilities, and working boats may also be seen. The building against the bridge (on the towpath side) has odd eye-shaped windows, and the corners of the bridge have grooves cut by towropes during the busy past. Bridge 24 has what looks like Christmas decorations hanging overhead, to stop swans flying into the wires, and then on the far side there's a spillway into the Ryal Burn. On the right there's a row of cottages with gardens running down to the burn. The next bridge is a 1930s utilitarian red brick and iron structure for the A89, and Bridge 25 (Miss Margaret's Bridge) links housing schemes with steps onto the towpath as you head north, cross the Brox Burn, and reach the A899, the main Uphall–Broxburn road at a modern concrete bridge of no character. Turn right if you want Broxburn's town centre; and at the traffic lights in the centre, if not returning to this spot, turn left again to rejoin the canal as it leaves the town.

Broxburn has a wide range of shops, coffee houses and pubs, and is a friendly place despite a rather unpretentious appearance. It straggles along north of the Brox Burn, and grew rapidly with the shale oil industry.

Broxburn

Niddry Castle below one of the oil shale bings

In 1861 the population was 660, in 1891 it was 5,898. They were either affy wild or unco guid in Victorian times. I lost count of the churches along the long High Street that joins it with Uphall. The West Church is 'weird and wonderful Gothic', and the Roman Catholic church the real showpiece. St Nicholas Parish Church, on the B8046 out of Uphall, is the only old church. Uphall was once Strathbrock (valley of badgers) and Broxburn is from the same old word, *brock* for badger (hence 'badger stream'). Uphall is a name which seems to cause pronunciation problems for some reason. It is just as written, Up hall, but people will produce 'Uffle' and such like. The Earl of Buchan built his solar-system model at the family home, Kirkhill. The family was connected with the area until after the Second World War. Broxburn's Roman Catholic church was built in 1880 for the Dowager Countess of Buchan. Its font has had a varied history. Dating to pre-Reformation times, it was ejected from the new kirk and for some time was used as a cattle water trough on a local farm. When it was recognised for what it was, the farmer gave it to the countess, who then presented it to the church.

Resuming the canal route, the A899 bridge leads to the wide Port Buchan basin, with seats, landscaping, picnic tables and toilets etc. Sheltered housing makes this a pleasant corner, then the canal swings to the northeast, between housing and various works, to reach Greendykes Road Bridge (27) which had to be rebuilt – in the Millennium style – to open the canal again. The red shale bings are now immediately ahead. (The word 'bing' has its derivation in the Gaelic 'ben' meaning a hill.)A launching and mooring wharf and car park is passed. The next two bridges are basically derelict, but the bing across the water bears the marks of adventurous bikers although, surprisingly, there are likely to be tits working through the alder and willow planting, moorhens fussing in the canal, swans gliding by and foxgloves colonising the slopes beyond. A high percentage of the foxgloves are white, maybe due to the poverty of the soil or its chemical composition. Further along the canal are banks of scented stock. (In September the slopes of the bing chitter with the sound of exploding broom pods.) A canal is often an artery of life in an otherwise lifeless landscape.

The brick-red colour of the bings is hardly surprising, for much of this spoil has been turned into bricks, or used for land reclamation at Grangemouth, or for motorway construction. Shale oil manufacturing was a typical Victorian enterprise. James 'Paraffin' Young first came to West Lothian in search of 'cannel coal' (candle coal – used for lighting as it burned with such a bright flame), and this led him to develop a process to extract paraffin oil and wax from the oil-bearing shales. So the oil industry began here. At its peak there were 120 works employing 13,000 people, but by 1873 the number had dropped to 30 as the oil wells of the USA began to produce their black gold. Young died in 1883, and the last works closed in 1962. 'Paraffin' Young was a chemical engineer from Glasgow. A fellow student who became a lifelong friend was David Livingstone, and much of the sponsorship for the latter's travels came from Young. Queen Victoria may have had the Falls on the Zambesi named after her, but there is a branch of the Lualaba named Young River. In this quiet setting (aircraft permitting), it is hard to imagine the atmosphere 150 years ago when dozens of chimneys poured smoke into the air. Grangemouth today is quite modest in comparison to its appearance in pictures of the old oil industry. The Almond Valley Heritage Centre in Livingston has a museum on the shale industry (as well as a mill, working farm, etc) and is worth a visit.

There's a pleasant open stretch with the bing passed. Away on the left is another which is jokingly referred to as Ayers Rock. Niddry Castle lies ahead, below yet another bing mountain. Winchburgh can be reached by walking past the castle as well as by keeping to the towpath, so a brief note on both. As the canal swings left (with Bridge 30 in sight) leave the towpath for the minor road. This crosses the main Edinburgh–Glasgow railway line (Broomhouse Bridge) and a glimpse over the parapet shows a cutting far deeper than the canal's. (The line continues through a tunnel under Winchburgh.) Turn left once over the bridge on the drive leading to the Castle. This bold tower sits somewhat incongruously in the middle of a golf course (with some modern defences against golf balls rather than cannon balls). The castle has had impressive restoration. It was built by the Seton family in 1490. Lord Seton was one of those who helped Mary Queen of Scots escape from Loch Leven Castle, and she was brought to Niddry briefly, before the battle of Langside led to her final flight and imprisonment in England. One of her 'Four Marys' (attendants) was Mary Seton. Mary Queen of Scots was three times as long a prisoner of Elizabeth as she was a free monarch in Scotland. The castle was sold in 1676 and abandoned early the next century.

Skirt the castle on the right (east) to drop down onto Niddry Castle Golf Course, and cross to walk up to Winchburgh on a woodland path outside the perimeter of the golf course and below the shale 'mountain'. The path comes out at the car park for the golfers, and the road up to the main street passes classic 1890s miners' 'rows'. En route, you can turn right to climb the bing through Hank Hill Wood, and it is worth wandering up this artificial hill for the view, and to see how nature is slowly greening-over the barren waste. The bings are beginning to be positive rather than negative features in the landscape. I trust some will be allowed to survive, both as wildlife sanctuaries and monuments to an important industry. Winchburgh had a brickworks which used the shale waste and was sending loads into Edinburgh by canal up till 1937 – the last real commercial use of the canal.

Keeping to the towpath to reach Winchburgh, the next bridge, 30, requires some caution from motorists, being humped, narrow and with sharp bends. The Niddry Burn comes out from under the canal, having risen near Beecraigs Country Park and entering the Almond at Kirkliston. Bell's Mill Wharf Bridge, 31, is the home of the Bridge 19–40 Canal Society and is dated 1820. Just before it, a path angles up to the road into town but is best ignored. A deep cutting follows with a modern pedestrian bridge (pipeline under) linking housing on the west bank with the town centre. Bridge 32 carries the B9080 road to Linlithgow and has had a tubular footbridge added on the south side. Go through under the bridge, and steps angle up to the road. Turn left for the town.

*Winchburgh
War Memorial*

TO THE GLORY OF HIM WHO DIED FOR ALL
AND TO THE MEMORY OF THOSE WHO FELL
IN BOTH WORLD WARS

1914 World War One 1918

WOII J W Lees MM	PTE John McWilliam
SGT John Lamb	PTE James Bann
SGT George M Coyle	PTE Charles Bann
L/CPL Andrew G Tweedhope	PTE Patrick Bann
L/CPL John Wilson	PTE Bernard Cochrane
L/CPL Thomas Thomson MM	PTE David Symons
L/CPL David Greenshields	PTE William Trotter
L/CPL Neil O'Donnell	PTE John C Peden

On the left, 120 metres on, is the Tally Ho, a substantial red sandstone building. Inside this inn are many photographs of Winchburgh in the days when the oil and brickworks were in full operation. On the other side there is a delightful war memorial figure of a drummer boy. An architectural guide points out 'in the village, a pompous Police Station', which has a splendid dragon on the 'gully box' (start of downpipe from guttering); it is now a pharmacy. A carved bird and the date 1903 adorn the Star and Garter. A few shops offer the chance of supplementary snacks.

4

Winchburgh to Linlithgow
OSLR 65; OSE 350, 349

More intriguing names in the area: Lampkinsdub, Paddockhall, Mounthooly, Cauldcoats, Totleywells, Tar Hill … Once down the steps onto the towpath there's one of several barriers to discourage motorcycles. A sign notes '6 miles to Linlithgow'; many consider these miles to Linlithgow the most serene and pleasing of all, as much is tree-lined and the noise of parallel rail lines and the M9 is muted.

A cottage on the far side has landscaped its portion of canal; Bridge 33 (Myre Bridge) only leads a track over to fields (a compensatory bridge), and in the deep-set stretch beyond there is the stage post for Sections 2 and 3, along with a battered old milestone (illustrated, page xix). Bridge 34 carries a track on a concrete way built on original abutments, with various tracks used by local walkers. Over the bridge, off the path up to the Winchburgh–Linlithgow road, lie the ruined gables of ancient Auldcathie Church. The name Priestinch points to a long-vanished pre-Reformation parish hereabouts.

Bridge 35, Craigtoun Bridge, is rather grander, with railings and ornamentation, as befits a one-time drive on the Hopetoun Estate. Bridge 36 is an estate bridge too, and from it a track goes up a steeply inclined bridge to pass over the railway. There are kicking stones again by the sturdier Bridge 37 which goes 'nowhere to nowhere'.

Bridge 38 at Fawnspark has been strengthened and given lights to cope with heavy commuter traffic. There's a car park beside it but the exit is onto a blind bend; highly dangerous. The canal then runs deeply through what feels like a cutting, as the waste from the shale oil industry is piled up on both sides – a wooded area much enjoyed by mountain bikers. Abutments show where a bridge connected with the industry once stood. Bridge 39 is now only used by cross-country walkers (a path from the Philpstoun road south to Threemiletown), but is worth going up onto for an attractive view, including a major overspill just west of Bridge 39. Good open, rural walking continues all the way to Linlithgow.

Westing from Winchburgh;
towards Bridge 35

A bit of fencing shows where a road is going under the canal – and the road itself crosses a burn. A mere hamlet now, Philpstoun was a place entirely dependent on the oil industry. The name dates back to Philip d'Eu, a 12th-century Norman who was granted land here. Various access paths lead up from the village and, on leaving, semicircular masonry walling marks a water-filled underpass linking fields.

After a slow transformation, the canal, from being deep in its private jungle, now runs along high, open country with fantastic views over the rolling Lowlands to the swelling Ochils on the northern skyline. The tower on the hill to the north is above The Binns, home of Tam Dalyell, the one-time local MP. An ancestor of the same name was a general, and a feared persecutor of the Covenanters. He was captured at the battle of Worcester, later reorganised the Russian army for the Tsar, won the battle of Rullion Green (1666) and raised the Scots Greys in 1681. They wore a grey cloth imported from the Netherlands, which the general had ordered to try and make his men less conspicuous in the field (a use of camouflage that was not in general practice for another 200 years!) His portrait shows stern features and a huge white beard. He scandalised society by never wearing boots.

Overlooking the Forth Estuary beyond The Binns is ancient Blackness Castle and the palatial Hopetoun House, all worth visiting. There are caravans by Bridge 40, and to the south is Campfleurie House, a French name. Continuing, there is a spread of allotments on the south side.

Kingscavil's Park Bridge, number 41, was the site of one of the change houses along the canal. The name means the 'King's plot of land' but the house and estate once belonged to the Hamiltons; young, newly-wed, cheery Patrick Hamilton was to be burnt at the stake in 1528 as the first Protestant martyr of the Reformation. In 1745, Prince Charles slept in the old house while his army lay at Threemiletown (Scots miles, longer than English). The bridge's number 41 has weathered away, and there are deep rope grooves on the bridge corners. There are visitors' moorings, and a launching slip on the far side. There is plenty of parking and the attractive Park Bistro across the road. Fishermen are often seen along this stretch and, even within the Edinburgh or Glasgow city boundaries, may land perch, roach, pike, bream, tench, carp or eels, testimony to the canal's clean water. Abutments show where a bridge once crossed the canal.

As you near Linlithgow, you are passing below Pilgrim Hill, and the name St Magdalene was once that of a fair and a hospice on the town's outskirts. The town has spilled out eastwards in a huge, impersonal suburb, Springfield. After Bridge 42, however, you have the Palace and St Michael's

Church in view. The canal passes over the B9080 as the town is reached (black and white railings). Below is what looks like a distillery with its pagoda-like towers, features which have been carefully preserved in turning the one-time St Magdalene distillery into houses. The 1960s saw much of historic interest swept away by an unimaginative local council, so this is a contrast. Liking or loathing is the reaction to the 1964 aluminium crown of thorns on top of St Michael's Kirk beside the Palace.

You come to the bowed parapet of another lane going under the canal. Immediately below is the station, and nearby was the site of the Nobel Works built in 1701, the Explosives Factory as it became in the World Wars. ICI purchased the works and then closed them down in the 1960s.

The grassy area below the castle is called the Peel, there being such a defence long before stone castles were built. Originally the canal builders had hoped to make use of the nearby loch, but the need to keep to its contour prevented that. Long staging leading to Bridge 43 marks a pioneering scheme to encourage permanent residence on the canal. Beyond Bridge 43 lies the attractive Manse Basin. At Bridge 43 and at the west end of the basin, white-painted slots indicate stop locks where bulks of wood (like sleepers) can be inserted to form dams so a stretch of canal (or this basin) could be dried out for maintenance work.

Manse Basin, Linlithgow

Teatime: on a St. Magdalene LUCS cruise

Here too the corners of the bridge have been deeply worn into grooves by tow ropes. The canal comes to life with a tearoom, museum and a collection of boats, the creation of LUCS, the Linlithgow Union Canal Society, an enthusiastic body of volunteers who have done much to revitalise this section of the canal, tidying the area, upgrading the towpath, rescuing everything old and interesting, running local trips in the *Victoria*, or perhaps to the Avon Aqueduct or the Wheel in the *St Magdalene*. The longboat *Leamington* can be chartered.

The museum, in the old stables building, is a fascinating record of the canal's past. Henry Bell of *Comet* fame was born in Linlithgow. The sprawl of Linlithgow below the canal is worth some exploration, as is the hill country above, and these are described in the next two chapters. The description of the continuation westwards along the Union Canal resumes in Chapter 7.

5

Linlithgow, Town of Black Bitches
OSLR 65; OSE 349

"When, on a summer evening about the hour of eight, I first beheld Dreamthorp, with its westward-looking windows painted by sunset, its children playing in the single straggling street, the mothers knitting at the open doors, the fathers standing about in long white blouses, chatting or smoking; the great tower of the ruined castle rising high into the rosy air, with a whole troop of swallows skimming about its rents and fissures; when I first beheld all this, I felt instinctively that my knapsack might be taken off my shoulders, that my tired feet might wander no more, that at last, on the planet, I had found a home. From that evening I have dwelt here, and the only journey I am like now to make, is the very inconsiderable one, so far at least as distance is concerned, from the house in which I live to the graveyard beside the ruined castle."

That comes from a book written in Victorian times by Alexander Smith, who is better known for a second book *A Summer in Skye*. The name, 'Dreamthorp', that he coined for the town, gave the Royal Burgh of Linlithgow one of its nicknames rather than anonymity. Smith died in 1867 when only 37.

Defoe thought Linlithgow 'a pleasant, handsome, well-built town' where bleaching linen was the obvious industry. Robert Burns was less flattering, saying Linlithgow 'carries the appearance of rude, decayed, idle grandeur' but thought it 'sweetly situated', William and Dorothy Wordsworth stopped off there for breakfast on the way to Edinburgh and the Borders at the end of their Highland Tour but made no particular comment.

For centuries Linlithgow was an important leather-making centre and so, like Selkirk, could be somewhat smelly. All the traditional industries have gone, though they are commemorated in the various guilds with their deacons. Linlithgow still elects a Provost; and the people of the town, regardless of sex, are Black Bitches. A black bitch appears on the town's

The crown of St. Michael's Church, Linlithgow

coat of arms. There are actually two coats of arms, the second portraying St Michael having a go at the dragon.

King David I built a house here in the 12th century, but like most Border or Central towns it suffered from the visits of English armies. They burnt the town in 1424. But with the Stuarts came prosperity. James I began the building of the palace and most of his successors added to it. Mary Queen of Scots was born in the palace in 1542. When James VI became James I in 1603 and flitted to London, this became a neglected second home.

Cromwell used it as barracks for nearly a decade. Later, it hosted Bonnie Prince Charlie, but was finally gutted after being occupied by Butcher Cumberland's troops. In 1989 Linlithgow celebrated the 600th anniversary of receiving its charter from Robert II, at the time when, in England, the Black Prince's son was king and Chaucer was penning his tales.

The following basic walkabout takes in most worthwhile features. From Manse Basin you look over to the Learmonth Gardens with a 16th-century beehive-type doocot holding 370 boxes. It has the standard stone courses sticking out to prevent rats climbing up, and a tiny door. Pigeons were popular in mediaeval times as they provided fresh meat in winter. Only nobles (Ross of Halkeld in this case) were allowed such; the common people just had old salted beef. There were no root crops then for winter feeding, so each autumn animals were slaughtered or driven south to English markets.

Turn east from the garden to go down a road, barred to traffic, which leads to the High Street after passing under the railway and by the station (on the Edinburgh–Glasgow/Stirling lines). The station was modernised in 1985 and opened by the well-known local MP Tam Dalyell. There's a colourful mural in the upper hall, worth seeing. Linlithgow had an ancient right to levy tolls, which it did on roads and then on the canal. The railway, however, refused to pay and despite various courts upholding the town, the House of Lords finally favoured no tolls for railways.

The road comes out onto the High Street near the one-time High Port, beside the welcoming Star and Garter Hotel, a black and white confection rather like an English coaching inn. Dating back to 1760 it was gutted by fire in 2010 and restored. Head left along the High Street, a hotchpotch of styles and periods with an unfortunate flat-roofed view-stopper to the east. A weathered figure of St Michael with the town's coat of arms stands on one of the many old wells, dated 1720 and inscribed 'St Michael is kinde to straingers'.

Across the High Street are several 16th- and 17th-century houses. The Hamilton Lands were restored by the National Trust for Scotland in 1958. Two have gables facing the street, with steep pantiles. Crowstep gables were designed to allow beams to be placed across a roof which was too steep for ordinary construction work. Behind one of the houses is an old outdoors baker's oven, from the days when fire was a serious hazard, and on the wall at the back of a pend is an inscription 'Ve Big Ye Se Varly 1527'. (*We build you see warily*.) At one time the town house of the Cornwalls of Bonhard stood here. An Alexander Cornwall was said to have been one of six knights dressed as look-alikes of the king – all of them, including the real James IV, killed at Flodden.

Along the road, the bulky Victoria Hall, completed in 1889, once had big Gothic towers and pepperpot turrets, but the building has failed steadily – the towers gone, turned into a cinema, then bingo hall, amusement arcade and now boarded up. On the south side still, above the sign of The Four Marys, is a tablet commemorating a Dr Waldie, who introduced chloroform to Sir James Simpson and the medical profession. At 79 High Street, between the first and second storey windows, is an early C19 'firemark' which indicated to firemen that the building was covered by fire insurance with the Sun Fire Office!

Continuing, the council building has a splendid example of a provost's lamp. The next building, the former Sheriff Court, has a tablet commemorating the assassination of the Regent Moray in 1570. Unfortunately it manages to spell Moray incorrectly and also gives the wrong date. This murder was one of the first- ever such deeds using a firearm and was very carefully prepared. Hamilton of Bothwellhaugh, after firing the shot, made his escape to the continent and, cashing in on the deed, became a professional hit-man. The archbishop, whose house he had used, was hanged.

The town centres round the Cross Well. The cross (a weekly market site) and gibbet have long gone, and the well has had a chequered history, being rebuilt in 1659 after damage from Cromwell's troops. In 1807 it was completely rebuilt, copying the old design, the work being done by a one-handed stonemason. The original Town House (Burgh Halls) was also destroyed by Cromwell, but rebuilt by the king's master mason John Mylne in 1668. Fire damaged it in 1847, when its Italian-style arched portico was replaced by popular wrought ironwork. The present double stairway superseded this in 1907. The Burgh Halls have a Tourist office, café (with garden) and Arts Centre.

Annet House, 143 High Street, a Georgian merchant house, is a Heritage Centre with a museum (life-sized models, memorabilia and video shows), and a restored garden in the rear 'rig'. (Open Apr–Oct)

The Kirkgate leads up from the Cross to reach the Palace gateway. Panels above have the gilded coats of arms of the Orders of the Garter, the Golden Fleece, St Michael (all conferred on James V) and the Thistle (which James V is thought to have founded). The porch at Abbotsford was based on this entrance – Walter Scott also cribbed bits of Melrose Abbey and Stirling Castle, quite apart from acquiring original old features.

Annet House Museum, the garden view

Through the arch, on the right, is St Michael's Parish Church, a large, cathedral-like building with a long history. Dedicated in 1242, most of it dates to a rebuilding after the 1424 fire. Its main fame is perhaps the window tracery, notably in the St Katharine's Aisle where James IV saw the ghost (a put-up by his worried wife?) who warned of impending doom if he marched an army south – to Flodden, as it proved. The Reformation took its toll of the decorative statuary. Cromwell actually quartered his troopers and their horses inside the church, and it accommodated Edinburgh students during the plague winter of 1645–46. There's a mortsafe lid still lying on the south side, in a walled enclosure.

The Creation Window is dedicated to Sir Wyville Thomson, the leader of the C19 *Challenger* Expedition which explored the world's oceans, and the huge window depicts a vast range of animals, birds and fish. Most heart-rending is the story behind the Child Samuel window, which commemorates the little daughter of a previous minister who died when her hair caught fire as she dried it before a blazing fire in the Manse. A sister had previously died when she went through the ice while skating on the loch with her fiancé. (The window hides behind the organ.)

Linlithgow Palace's most famous tale is its capture for Robert the Bruce by a local farmer, William Binnie, who regularly used to deliver hay to the garrison. One day he hid men under the hay and stopped the cart in the entrance so the portcullis and gates couldn't operate. More men rushed in, and the palace was won.

The impressive feature of Linlithgow Palace (in the care of Historic Scotland) is its courtyard fountain which has been fully restored: tiers of symbols and figures exquisitely carved – as are the recent replacements. The setting, too, is grand. It was Mary of Guise who declared she had "never seen a more princely palace".

The Palace stands in what is collectively called The Peel which, like Falkland Palace, is still a royal park. To walk round the loch – which gives fine views to palace, church and town – takes about an hour. Two of the loch's islets are artificial, being crannogs (loch dwellings of about 5,000 years ago). Yellow water lilies have flowered in the loch for centuries, and it is a bird sanctuary, sometimes with wintering swans gathering in hundreds. At the period when the palace was being used, gardens, orchards and an apiary surrounded it, and the loch would provide water for brewing as well as fish, eels, ducks and swans for eating. When Bonnie Prince Charlie marched in, the fountain was reputedly spouting wine! The town once had about ten wells, hence its part in the jingle:

> *Glasgow for bells*
> *Linlithgow for wells,*
> *Falkirk for beans and peas*
> *Peebles for clashes and lees.*

The West High Street has less historic interest, but provides several more cafés and restaurants with which the town is well supplied. If followed to the end, Preston Road, running south, leads up to the Union Canal at the restored Bridge 45, from which Beecraigs is also reached; described in the next chapter.

6

Beecraigs, Cockleroy and Cairnpapple
OSLR 65; OSE 349

South of Linlithgow lie the Bathgate Hills, as they tend to be called, and they have three notable sites worth visiting, either afoot from Linlithgow or, quite feasible, by taxi: a country park (with a red deer herd), a notable wee hill with a big view and one of Scotland's finest prehistoric sites. The last really needs one's own transport but is briefly mentioned here, while Beecraigs Country Park and Cockleroy give some verticality as an alternative to the constant contoured level of the canal!

The best approach is up from Bridge 45, Preston Road Bridge, reached from the west end of the High Street or by walking along the towpath from the Manse Basin. When Preston Road reaches the edge of town there's a good path for walkers, cyclists, horse-riders and energetic wheelchair users, running parallel with the road to give safe access to the Hillhouse Woods and Beecraigs. Many gates allow farm access to fields, and when the route turns left, eastwards, a map board describes the woodland stretching ahead.

The path steadily rises and gives opportunity for tree recognition games; there's Scots pine, larch and other conifers, oak, ash, sycamore, beech, gean (sweet cherry), rowan, hazel and elder. Keep to the gritty path (ignore any grassy options). After yet another gate an old quarry (right) is passed where the path becomes wide enough for vehicles. An open grassy area is reached, with swathes of rosebay willowherb in summer and an all-year east–west view on a grand scale. The path loops round and back, to eventually run parallel to a minor road which is joined at a junction, with Beecraigs signed. (From the panoramic area there's a bench above the track, and behind it a grassy path heads more directly up to the exit of Hillhouse Wood.)

Head down the tarred road past the restaurant (open for lunches, dinners) and caravan site entrance, and the Visitor Centre is off left, a log cabin structure with a grass roof. Minimal refreshments are available. Local displays, maps and park information. From the far corner of the car park there is a raised walkway giving a view over the farm fields and off to the green swelling of the Riccarton Hills – not to be taken for Cockleroy. The path goes through the fields so there's clear observation of the Highland cattle, Belted Galloways and red deer. The red deer are not tame animals but are farmed commercially just like cattle or sheep, or like the trout at the fish farm beside Beecraigs Loch where you come out. Rainbow trout are reared, may be fed, and purchased for supper. Turn left to follow the shore round and over the dam, below which lies the fish farm.

The park has a wide range of activities: field archery, orienteering, fishing, cycling, horse-riding, trim course, climbing wall, etc. The loch is well hidden among conifer woodlands with Dagger Island covered in Scots pine and looking like something out of Arthur Ransome. Near the west end of the circuit, a board lists ducks galore, coot, moorhen, greylag, swan and other birds. Exit across a minor road to Lochside car park.

From the entrance of the car park take the Balvormie footpath/forest track up through the trees to eventually reach the big Balvormie surfaced car park beside another minor road (play area off right). Cross it; there's a pond, left, and right, a sign for Cockleroy. You reach yet another minor road and the Cockleroy car park. From the far end of the car park (noticeboard) a path/track leads up a dark tree tunnel so there is a sharp contrast when you suddenly come out to the breezy open hillside beyond (gate/stile). A steep five-minute ascent lands you on the summit of Cockleroy with its

On top of Cockleroy

view indicator, trig point and 360-degree panorama which rates among the best in the Lowlands – from Bass Rock to Goat Fell is not bad for 278m (912ft) in the middle of the Lowlands.

The wide saddle of the Cauldstane Slap in the Pentlands, the rock fin of Binny Craig, the crouching lion shape of Arthur's Seat, the hunky stump of the Bass Rock, all lie to the east. Working anti-clockwise, the various Forth Bridges are well seen, the Lomonds are bold, behind Linlithgow are the Cleish Hills, then comes the long horizon of the Ochils. The big, high chimney is that of the Longannet Power Station. Grangemouth is a jungle of chimneys and cooling towers, and beyond is the Kincardine Bridge. (The dusk view when all these areas are lit up is quite spectacular.) Running away to the west are the Campsie Fells, while real Highland hills can also be seen: Ben Vorlich, Ben Ledi, Ben More (by Crianlarich), Ben Venue, Ben Lomond. Both Stirling and Edinburgh Castle can be seen. In the *Companion* days Falkirk's 'celebrated foundry of Carron' was 'distinguished by thick clouds of smoke' while the masts of the shipping indicated Grangemouth.

Nearer, below you to the south-west, is the obvious Lochcote Reservoir. Not so obvious, but between it and craggy Bowden Hill to the west, lies a flat area which was a loch until drained last century, when a crannog was discovered. Just to be different, Beecraigs Loch is man-made, built by prisoners of war during World War I. Both Cockleroy and Bowden Hill (229m/770ft) summits are the sites of prehistoric forts, though there is nothing much to see. Quite magnificent, however, is the excavated and preserved multi-period prehistoric henge, circles and tomb on Cairnpapple Hill, due south – one of the Top Ten prehistoric sites in Scotland – next to the obvious relay mast. The knobbly nature of these hills points to their volcanic origins.

The grassy depression on Cockleroy is called Wallace's Cradle. The patriot reputedly used the hill as an observation post and safe spot in the dangerous Lowlands, where most of his life was spent. He held a parliament at nearby Torphichen, another historic site well worth a visit.

Cockleroy is not a French hybrid word but murdered Gaelic, *cochull-ruadh*, the red cowl. (On an 1898 OS map it is Cocklerue, and an 18th-century guide had Cuckold le Roy.) In this 'waist of Scotland', not surprisingly, is a real mix of Gaelic, Norman and old British names – and some guid Scots one too, like Burghmuir or Cauldhame. Beecraigs is also Gaelic in origin, from *beithe* (pronounced bey) meaning birch tree.

To reach Cairnpapple Hill by car, turn right on leaving Beecraigs Visitor Centre, then left along by Hillhouse Wood (good view of Cockleroy), left, then right at a fork. Two kilometres on at a long layby, there's the Scottish Korean War Memorial to visit, then it's on, first left, first right, and a small parking area for Cairnpapple. The site is important enough to be open Apr–Sept, Sun, Mon, Tues, Fri with guided tours on Sun, Mon; to book, tel: 0131-550 7603. When the custodian is present you can climb down into the burial chamber of the central cairn, an unforgettable experience. Last time there I saw swallows, a wheatear and a kestrel hovering overhead while a skylark sang in the blue. Do add these joys to the canals travel.

7

Linlithgow to Polmont and Muiravonside Country Park
OSLR 65; OSE 349

As one heads west from the Manse Basin and its moorings, good views open up to St Michael's church with its crown of thorns and the historic palace. Bridge 44 is a rebuilt specimen, and Bridge 45 (Preston Road) is a pre-millennium reconstruction, carried out to allow Linlithgow-based boats to reach the Avon Aqueduct. 1991 saw the Preston Road culvert replaced by the present bridge. This also did away with the amusing but necessary red triangle warning sign on Preston Road depicting a swan; the culvert was too low for a swan's passage so they wandered across the road.

Bridge 46 is well out in the suburbs. Note how the Golf Course Road passes under the canal, the golf course lying south of the canal. A pipeline crosses as a complex 'bridge' and then there is an overspill. Near the end of the golf course another underpass heads south, up to what were quarries from which stone was shipped to Edinburgh for the building of the New Town. Over on the right is the Telford Avon railway viaduct with its 23 arches. The building of these viaducts owed much to the skills learned from constructing canal aqueducts so there's a deal of irony in the railways killing off the canals. The canals across Scotland were eventually bought by railway companies – which, irony on irony, kept them alive till the demands of road traffic not only forced the closure of the canals but also took most of the goods traffic from the railways as well.

During the canal's eclipse years, when it was technically a 'remainder' waterway, a stretch of canal here was sealed off and empty because of constant leaking. The 'Kettlestoun Breach' was tackled pre-Millennium by monies raised both locally and internationally, and I can recall the thrill of then being able to cruise on one of LUCS boats out to the Avon Aqueduct.

The next bridge has a wrong (and confusing) 45 carved on the east side, and 47, correctly, on the west. This is a much-repaired small bridge, and the A706 now runs close beside the canal. Just ahead is Woodcockdale, one of the old change houses where relays of horses for towing would be swopped over. The building has been well preserved and is used by Sea Cadets. The English-sounding Woodcockdale name has been found on a map of 1491. There are visitor moorings and a large car park just to the west, reached by driving down and along the towpath. Bridge 48 immediately after is a much-patched one, as the A706 Lanark road gives it a hammering. Under the bridge, on the south side, there is another 'stop gate', but as like as not these days truckloads of material are just dumped into the canal to form a barrier and the water pumped out.

There's a winding basin not far beyond Bridge 48, popular with swans. Any young swans are ringed and studied. In winter they tend to gather on Linlithgow Loch or on the eastern seaboard anywhere between Montrose Basin and Northumberland.

Steps coming up bring the River Avon Heritage Trail and the John Muir Trail onto the towpath (near a seat). Downstream these lead to Linlithgow Bridge, which offers another pleasant circular walk; and once across the Avon Aqueduct, the Heritage Trail continues upstream through Muiravonside Country Park to end at Avonbridge.

The John Muir Way runs from Dunbar to Helensburgh and periodically joins the Lowland canals (but, strangely, avoids the UC tunnel) so its signs will be seen periodically. John Muir was born in Dunbar but went to the USA with his autocratic father in 1849. He would go on to an eventful life as inventor, traveller, mountaineer, wilderness champion, shepherd, farmer and author. Check him out on the internet. Visit his birthplace in Dunbar. Join the John Muir Trust.

Past mooring rings and a bend, and you find yourself suddenly confronted by the canal's most spectacular engineering feature, the great Telford-inspired Avon Aqueduct. Only Telford's 1805 Pontcysyllte Aqueduct in Wales is larger in the whole of Britain. The 1823 *Companion* declares of the Avon Aqueduct: 'This noble edifice, which, for magnificence, is scarcely equalled in Europe, consists of twelve arches, is nearly 900 feet in length and 85 in height. The woody glens, the rugged heights, and the beautiful Alpine scenery around, must raise sensations of pleasure in every feeling heart.'

Downstream, visible beyond the tree-choked river, is the Telford Avon railway viaduct, now a Grade A listed structure. The Avon's waters drain from the Bathgate hills to the River Forth. On the river below here an old

Canoes on the Avon Aqueduct

priory was largely washed away by a single spate, so only a gable stands on the edge of the dell. In pre-glacial times the Avon flowed through what is now Linlithgow Loch to reach the sea at Blackness. Beyond the railway viaduct is the site of the Battle of Linlithgow Bridge, 1526, when the Earl of Lennox was killed after being captured in an abortive attempt to rescue the young James V (born in Linlithgow) from the clutches of the Earl of Angus, the head of the notorious Douglases. The Avon was much used for providing power, and past centuries saw several paper mills established. Walkers can look down on a weir when crossing the aqueduct (cyclists might prefer to walk too: very rough setts).

The aqueduct remains spectacular and, from below, is geometrically graceful. It was only possible thanks to Telford's ingenuity in using an iron trough to carry the water instead of the usual puddled (kneaded) clay, which was much heavier and just couldn't be carried on slender, practical arches. (Baird was able to build these arches hollow, with struts.) Once across, on the north side, if you go down a little, you'll see a grated opening which allows inspection access to the interior of the aqueduct. Inspectors can work along inside the structure.

If pioneering techniques went into building these canals, some of the ships to use them were historic. Henry Bell's famous *Comet*, the world's first practical seagoing steamship, was brought through from the Forth and Clyde Canal for her first overhaul at Bo'ness, where Bell had served his apprenticeship. The spectators fled the harbour as the *Comet* arrived; they had assumed from the smoke that the ship was on fire and might blow up at any moment.

Having crossed the mighty aqueduct it is only right to go down the 100-plus steps to view it from below – and then continue on a diversion that is highly recommended. This keeps to the south side of the canal, and also allows a visit to the Muiravonside Country Park. The canal towpath could then be rejoined by crossing Bridge 49 or 50, but the more interesting walking remains on the south side on to Bridge 51, altogether some of the best walking on the canals.

Before descending, look ahead and you'll see a rusty barge (too decayed to move) 'floating' in what was once a dry dock. The dock worked very simply, by just stopping the end next to the canal, and then releasing the water inside which drained down by a side stream into the Avon. Swans have continuously nested in the dock for many years. They eat floating duckweed which tends to accumulate in quiet waters like this. Along all the canals the biggest invader is sweet reed grass (*Glyceria maxima*), dominant, attractive, and a real pest. There's also an old milestone: 7 (to Falkirk), 24 (to Edinburgh). You'll notice how all the new milestones have kept to the same shape and script as the original, but will have an MM on the back. They were made by the apprentice masons of Historic Scotland. The stones were always angled so as to be easily read from passing traffic. The pillar next to the milestone is another of the four stage posts, the last if heading west and inscribed as 'betwixt the third and fourth stages' – if you can make out the words.

If you do just continue along the towpath (second best; the preferred options are described below) Bridge 49 is soon reached. It has had some remedial work, and access to the B825 lies 100 metres on from the bridge. Across the canal you will see the Bridge 49 Café/Bistro which might tempt – and then stay on that side along to Bridge 51. Just after, abutments show where yet again a bridge once stood: built after the canal and its purpose (industrial) becoming obsolete, the bridge disappeared. Bridge 50 is the Almond Bridge, and Bridge 51 the Vellore Road Bridge, a rebuilt one in the praiseworthy Millennium restoration style. The diversion to the better south side ends here, and the two south side options following the descent from the Avon Aqueduct are now described.

The quick and easy diversion first. Having descended and admired the impressive arches from the end of the steps/walkway turn right on a large track which crosses the Boyhouse Burn by a stone bridge and rises steadily. Keep right at a junction and soon join a drive out to the B825, close to Bridge 49 – and the Bridge 49 Café/Bistro.

Alternatively, from the end of the steps/walkway a longer circuit can be made to take in interesting features of the Muiravonside Country Park. Head straight on (passing a grotto) to join a motorable track which passes the Outdoor Learning Centre (part of the building is an old mill) to a wide

The huge spans of the Avon Aqueduct

grassy area. From its right edge a path climbs steadily up, crosses an old mill lade (or leat), and still up to meet a flight of steps. Turn down these (trail sign with the aqueduct symbol). Curiously the path goes through a small walled cemetery for the Victorian Stirling family, who once owned the Muiravonside estate. David Stirling of SAS fame was a more recent member of the family. (A striking statue of him stands looking towards the Highlands on the Bridge of Allan–Doune road.)

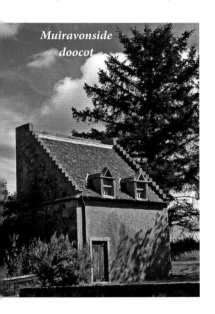

Muiravonside doocot

The path leads to the Steadings, the first feature of which is a fine doocot, one of the 'lectern' type. At Linlithgow we saw an earlier style, a 'beehive' doocot; these eventually gave way to rectangular buildings with a single sloping roof, imaginatively compared to a lectern in a church. The one here is a link with the third style which was purely ornamental, often as part of stable blocks or set on some eye-catching spot, really a folly rather than a way of meeting any need for pigeons as a food source.

There's a café at the Steadings Visitor Centre, but only open at weekends. Head along the drive but then take a path, right, to reach the big car park. Cross it diagonally to the road into Newparks Farm which has an impressive collection of beasts and birds on view (there's a list on a wall). There are also toilets. Go left round outside the farm, and cross paths to descend steps steeply to the Boyhouse Burn. Cross a footbridge and, left, is a fine old limekiln. Climb up to a meeting of paths, and take the second left, which soon joins a drive out to the B825, close to Bridge 49 – and just as close to Bridge 49 Café/Bistro.

Continuing on the south side, from the back of the café/bistro follow a path by the palings/beech hedge. This passes abutments of a one-time railway and leads to the restored Slamannan (or Causewayend) Basin, where there are moorings for temporary or residential use. Coal was once transferred to barges here, the lines jutting out over the basin, so when the doors were opened, the coal fell straight into the barges.

An old track leads on through woodland, an overgrown bing on the left, the canal on the right. After passing under a bridge (the road from

Bridge 50) the canal bank is rejoined for a delightful path along to Bridge 51. There are plenty of Scots pines, and many consider this the best of all sections of the Union Canal and the basin/moorings at Bridge 51 an idyllic spot. (There are picnic tables.) End of the southern diversion.

Heading off along the *towpath* from Bridge 51, you come to an overspill across the towpath with steps up and along by a burn to allow access to Muiravonside Church, where there's a large parking area. The old walled graveyard has a superb collection of 18th-century stones, many obviously by the same masons, craftsmen with a taste for fanciful supporting trumpeters, symbolic circles and other emblems of mortality and immortality – one of the best collections of this folk art, which neglect is steadily destroying.

Continue, once back at the overspill, to Kirk Bridge (Bridge 52), which seems to have been abandoned but is a good viewpoint for Stirling Castle, the Ochils and Saline Hills (pronounced *sal-in*), and with the familiar shapes of Ben Vorlich and Stuc a' Chroin visible. The extensive Manuel Works (refractories, terracotta products, and much else) lay beyond the graveyards, and in the middle of this sprawl is the square tower of Almond or Haining Castle, once a seat of the Earls of Linlithgow and Callendar, but derelict for over 200 years.

Rural walking leads on to a bridge which caused some problems over its restoration. Its number 52A indicates there wasn't a bridge here originally, so when the A801 was built to link the M9 with Bathgate and Livingstone the canal was just culverted. The problem was similar to the M8 nearing Broxburn, so here too the canal puts in an S bend. The A801 runs uphill, and on the original canal line there would not have been enough headroom to pass under the road, so the canal bent sharply left and right to pass under where there was headroom.

Bethankie Aqueduct is an example of where it's the canal that does the bridging. The feature is easily overlooked, as there is just a short curve of parapet. There's arch on arch – for while the canal spans the road, the road spans a burn!

There is a clear view across to the vast array of cooling towers and so on that mark Grangemouth, but they soon drop out of sight as you walk this open stretch, the railway in a cutting beside you and Polmont houses ahead. Despite the feeling of suburbia, only a farm track crosses Bridge 53, and you hardly see Polmont thereafter as you enter a hemmed-in cutting leading to the large span of Bridge 54 (Brightons Bridge). An iron pedestrian bridge has been added on the west side. There's a shop and other facilities near at hand, and also, Polmont station which, with others, makes walking

A gravestone in Muiravonside kirkyard

stretches of canal easy, as a return to a start can be made by train. (Polmont to Falkirk High or to Linlithgow are examples.) There's a plaque at Polmont station recalling the rail disaster of July 1984, when 13 people died and 61 were injured.

8

Polmont to the Falkirk Wheel
OSLR 65; OSE 349

From the Polmont bridge (No 54) there's access on both sides of the canal briefly, a winding hole moorings, and an overspill which goes into the Polmont Burn which flows under the canal. The burn joins the large Westquarter Burn, to head through Grangemouth into the sea at the docks. A concrete footbridge with blue railings links new housing with the town. The canal swings westwards with the view to the Ochils opening up again.

Approaching the ugly non-standard Bridge 55, there is staging on the far side of the canal where there's an outdoor pursuits complex, making use of the canal. To the north the railway out of Polmont divides, one branch heading to Stirling (via Falkirk Grahamstown) and the other, the canal-follower, heading to Glasgow (via Falkirk High). Redding Number 23 Pit once stood beside the canal, and was the scene of one of the worst mining disasters in Scotland on 25 September 1923; water from abandoned workings broke into the pit and 40 died. Five miners were brought out alive after nine days and it was nearly three weeks before rescue attempts were called off. In Old Polmont graveyard I found a heartbreaking stone that read, 'Colin Maxwell, aged 58 years. Also his two sons, Walter, aged 28 years and Colin, aged 17 years, who all died in the Redding Pit disaster ...'

There's a staging, facing the high concrete walling of a prison: Polmont Young Offenders Institute. Some sources suggest that the notorious Burke was a navvy in the Polmont area, others that he was working on the Falkirk tunnel when he met Hare, the two to ply their nefarious trade in Edinburgh. There's an accessible Tesco below the towpath.

Bridge 56 carries pipes across, and then comes the 'Canal Corridor' development with houses up on the south side, and swathes of grass running down to the canal, a long stretch of moorings (and an intake) and, to the north, the Redding Park Industrial Estate. For a while we walk along a road edging this estate. There's a big winding hole, and later a swing bridge

From Bridge 61 to Bridge 60
on the Union Canal

abandoned on the far side, which once gave access to chemical works. As the only swing bridge on the Union Canal, it deserves preservation. A travellers' site hidden by *Leylandii* hedging lies below the north side of the towpath.

Bridge 57 also carries pipes on brick pillars, and passing under the canal (not seen) is the large Westquarter Burn which bisects Grangemouth.

Bridge 58 is abandoned but from it the white geometric houses of Hallglen are starkly visible beyond the busy railway line which runs along below the canal. Bridge 59 (Huts Bridge) just leads to fields, and the canal banks are increasingly wooded again. A cobbled overspill (through a wall pierced with square holes) falls into the deep-set Glen Burn which runs into the Westquarter Burn. Shortly, curved walls show where the burn flows from under the canal. Bridge 60 spans our deep wooded walk, one of the biggest arches over the Union Canal. What isn't visible from the towpath is that the Glen Burn runs in a deep trench above and parallel to the canal. Bridge 61, Glen Bridge, has a second span, with neat curving parapets over the burn. Invisible from the canal, it is easy to walk up to and see.

Bridge 61 has a unique feature: there are carved faces on both keystones – that on the east laughing, that on the west glum and girning – and popularly known as the 'Laughing and Girning Bridge'. Accounts vary as to their meaning. Did one smile at the long miles built from the capital? Did the other grimace at the work just ahead in creating what was probably the first-ever transport tunnel in Scotland? It has also been suggested the masons showed their feelings for the characters of their respective bosses when the work met here. Above the faces are ovals with the Number 61 and the date 1821. Along the 100 yards leading on to the tunnel are excellent examples of kicking stones.

There was really no need for a tunnel, but the 18th-century industrialist William Forbes, who had bought Callendar House (forfeited from the Jacobite Livingstons) objected to the proposed route, as it would be in view from the palatial chateau he was making out of the old house. The building and its parklands now belong to Falkirk Council and there's a good stretch of the Antonine Wall's *vallum* (ditch) visible in the park. The park can be reached from Falkirk High railway station, described at the end of this chapter.

The 690-yard (631m) tunnel through Prospect Hill was quite a construction feat when you realise it was cut by navvies working with horses at best – and none of today's power tools. Three shafts were sunk so the tunnel could have several work faces operating at once. It was 18

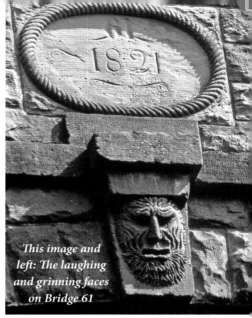

This image and left: The laughing and grinning faces on Bridge 61

A feature within the canal tunnel

The canal tunnel's eastern entrance

feet (5.5m) wide (13ft of waterway, 5ft of towpath) and a bit more in height (6½ft of water, 12ft clearance, total 19ft/6m). The tunnel is lit but still has a somewhat spooky atmosphere. There is a sturdy handrail for safety. Where water runs down the walls or drips from the roof some beautiful formations have been created. Lighting and/or towpath surface may be poor/wet so a torch is worth carrying. Just to the north the Edinburgh–Glasgow railway also runs through a tunnel, and a road goes over the exit.

You come out from the tunnel to a park-like area, with tidy grass verges and well-made paths, a signpost noting Polmont 4, Edinburgh 31½, Falkirk Wheel 2. Falkirk High station is just off to the right. There is a basin (fine overnight moorings) before the Bantaskine or Walker's Bridge (Number 62) – which is the last). A nice moment comes when the screening on the right finishes and there is a clear view of the hills: Campsies (left), the cone of Ben Ledi, Ben Vorlich and Stuc a' Chroin, and the bulky Ochils. By Bridge 62 the Seagull Trust's *Govan Seagull* (built by Govan shipbuilders in 1984) operates from a reception centre in Bantaskine Park, allowing disabled visitors to sail through the tunnel or out to the Falkirk Wheel. The *Barr Seagull*, built in Falkirk, was added to the Seagull Trust fleet in 2006. The woodland park has attractive paths and a quiet ambience.

The canal continues along above Falkirk to a milestone with '½ mile' on one side indicating the original distance to the end of the canal. Beyond, at a basin with moorings and a slip, an incut on the right marks a historical spot, though there is virtually nothing to see today except a dirt track running down to the road that went under the massive arches of the railway viaduct. Having dutifully kept to its 240-foot contour line all the way from Edinburgh, the Union Canal ended 112 feet above the Forth & Clyde Canal so, perforce, they were linked by a flight of locks, no less than 11 of them, down the line of this dirt track, to a large basin, Port Downie, (named from an investor Robert Downie of Appin) beside Lock 16 of the Forth & Clyde Canal. The attractive Georgian Union Inn took its name from this historical spot, and at least the inn's welcoming presence still survives. Old photos show the flight of locks swinging under a six-arched railway viaduct but, at the time (1961) of filling in the locks and creating roads, this was replaced by the high railway bridge there now.

Let me indulge in a personal note here. I was once trying to photograph the Union Inn and the locks on a showery day and was constantly in and out of my camper van during the mini deluges. With a variety of doors the inevitable happened: I found I'd locked myself out. After some thought I went in to the inn and, all too audibly, asked the barman for the loan of a

Part of the original flight of eleven locks from the Union Canal down to join the Forth & Clyde Canal

The Union Inn

bar stool, a broom and a wire coat hanger. This caused a speculative hush, and when I carried out my collection of objects I was followed by most of the drinkers, obviously curious to see what was afoot. Well, the stool let me climb onto the Transit's roof where I lifted open a skylight through which I was able to insert the broom, at the end of which I had fashioned a hook from the wire coat hanger. Very carefully I hooked the bunch of keys lying on the sink draining board and drew them through the skylight. Success was greeted by a polite round of applause.

Alternative plans to connect the Union Canal with the Forth & Clyde Canal, mooted by Robert Stevenson and Thomas Telford, were to carry it on to the Wyndford lock on the F & C Canal, but several locks would still be needed and another big aqueduct across the Castlecary 'gap', as well as cutting more miles of canal. There's an element of sadness in the disappearance of the splendid flight down to Port Downie.

Which, of course, set a big problem over linking the two canals again. Reinstating the original line was no longer practicable: roads, buildings and a town's infrastructure ruled that out. So what was to be done? The answer was bold and ingenious – the Falkirk Wheel: a rotary boat lift which would simply pick up a boat from the higher level and gently lower it to the basin below (or vice versa). To make room for this the Union Canal was extended; so, after a look at the spot where the flight broke off, we can push on for the unique Falkirk Wheel.

Continue to a Y-junction of the canal: the short section left is the original ending of the Union Canal (an 1823 extension, Port Maxwell, from which passengers *walked* down to Port Downie – it could take many hours for a boat to descend the linking eleven locks). The right fork, the new continuation, is another MM creation, Summerford Aqueduct, which strides across a road twisting up underneath (the road climbs up to the monument on the site of a 1746 battle, of which more later) and heads on westwards. A last contact with the railway is made on this high towpath. The next bridge has no towpath going under it, so we go up and over. A concrete bridge (Lime Bridge) comes in, right, from the Tamfourhill houses, and the track off left is taken by the John Muir Trail. Back to the canal gives a rare (brief) free-wheeling for cyclists, a wider maintenance track leading to the final features of the Union Canal.

There is staging, then two deep locks down to a basin (note Santa's Grotto!), then the canal swings northwards, vanishing into the 180-metre Rough Castle tunnel, which passes under the Edinburgh–Glasgow railway, a road (Camelon–High Bonnybridge) and the line of the Roman Antonine Wall,

Swans by the old Port Maxwell extention; left

Heading towards the top of the Falkirk Wheel

to come out right onto the Falkirk Wheel aqueduct – a great effect. There's a stone bench and a memorial to Campbell Christie. One can walk down to the Visitor Centre or follow a path up and over the tunnel entrance to go down the other side (passing the path to Rough Castle fort on the Roman Wall).

The striking image of the Falkirk Wheel is on a par with the Kelpies or the Forth Bridge, yet the practical operating of the lift system is basically simple. There are two balancing gondolas (one with boat or boats on board) which are set in motion so as one descends the other goes up. So fine is this balance that the electricity needed costs less than £20 a day. But the joy of this creation is the marriage of engineering with what can only be described as art; architecture as sculpture, practical inspiration into instant icon. The two Scottish Canals tour boats which go up the lift, along through the tunnel and back (1 hour) are named *Antonine* and *Archimedes*.

The Visitor Centre itself is of bold design and has various displays, café and gift shop, and there's a working model of the Wheel.

The large basin-cum-marina, New Port Downie, has all the facilities for canal users and is joined to the Forth & Clyde Canal by the Jubilee Lock.

The Falkirk Wheel in operation

On the far side of the basin are moorings and an extensive grassy picnic area with food available, a Children's Activity Zone with a Water Park (with an Archimedes screw to work). An excellent 1–2 hour circular walk can be made from the Wheel to visit Rough Castle, the Roman Fort on the Antonine Wall, and this, with other options, is described in Chapter 11.

A signposted path leads to a rotating footbridge across the Forth & Clyde Canal to make the final walkers' link of the two canals. What next? Perhaps the circular walk to the Roman fort, most definitely the descent to the Helix Park and the spectacular Kelpies – a duty anyway if intending to follow the Forth and Clyde Canal from sea to sea.

9

Falkirk Town
OSLR 65; OSE 349

The slopes above UC Bridge 62 saw the last Jacobite success of the Forty-Five rising, just three months before Culloden. There is nothing to see on the ground, and the roadside monument (NS 867789) is a crude concrete obelisk. The story is not without interest though. Lord George Murray surprised Hawley, who was camped at Falkirk, and drove his force back to Edinburgh. The clash occurred on a windy, sleety day in January 1746. The Livingstons, Earls of Linlithgow, had Jacobite leanings and their estates were forfeited after the Fifteen but the Falkirk 'Bairns' (as the town folk are still called) refused to pay rent to the York Building Company and the estate was leased back to the Countess of Kilmarnock, the Livingstons' heiress, whose husband had 'come out' for Prince Charles, was captured and beheaded. Ironically, Hawley, leader of the government forces, was dining with the countess when the Jacobites attacked his forces.

Callendar House (described below) saw most of the regular figures of note: Mary Queen of Scots, Cromwell (it was Monck's Scottish HQ) and Charles Edward Stuart, en route for Derby. One of the unenthusiastic participants in the 1746 battle was the Gaelic poet Duncan Ban MacIntyre, who is forever linked with Ben Dorain. An earlier Livingston was principal guardian of Mary Queen of Scots, and the nobles at Callendar House in Falkirk had to decide if Mary and Edward, son of Henry VIII, should be betrothed. They decided no, and Mary went off to France for safety. One of her 'Four Marys' was Mary Livingston.

The first bloody battle of Falkirk was back in the time of the Wars of Independence, and was the sad end to Wallace's efforts to free Scotland from English interference. He had finally succeeded in driving out all the English garrisons, had been appointed 'Guardian of Scotland' and carried fire and sword into Northern England. Edward I was in Flanders fighting the French king, but was forced to return and invade Scotland in 1298. Wallace's smaller, less-trained force was caught at Falkirk and, despite bloody resistance, was simply massacred by the sheer weight of English numbers and the deadly longbow which weakened the 'schiltrons' of fierce spearsmen. Wallace continued the struggle, went in vain for continental support and, on his return, was betrayed. Edward had him barbarously hung, drawn and quartered as a 'traitor' which ensured he has been a national hero ever since.

This central corridor of the country was much fought over, for Stirling was the lowest bridging point on the Forth and so forced communications in that direction, for good or ill. We seldom remember how greatly history is affected by geography, both in the big events and battles and in everyday social activity and trade. Falkirk as the 'epicentre of Scotland' could hardly escape. Now it is a town of 40,000 inhabitants and a busy place despite the decline of older industries. Coal mines and iron foundries made it a leader in the Industrial Revolution.

It was an East Lothian entrepreneur who began this industrial revolution, but his local mine owner would not reduce prices to make production viable. The famous Abyssinian traveller, Bruce of Kinnaird, had pits near Falkirk and he delivered the goods. So Carron, now swallowed up by Falkirk, became the heavy iron industry centre of Scotland with the biggest ironworks in Europe in 1814. Hark to the *Companion's* description of the reality. 'In daylight, the thick columns of rising smoke, with the flames bursting through them at intervals, and the high chimneys, with the sable hue of the far extended brick buildings, present a grand but gloomy scene, which is strongly contrasted with the green woods around and the artificial sheets of water collected for the use of machinery. But, if night, the prospect is terribly sublime – the huge flames issuing from the furnaces – the charring coals spread out like sheets of fire – and the luminous circle that spreads around the whole, joined to the noise arising from the clanking of the chains, and the roaring of the bellows, presents such a noble and terrific scene ...'

That has all passed away. Roman camps, town walls and old buildings have all gone but many 18th-century buildings are now carefully preserved, there is an excellent museum and a rebuilt town centre (much glass and concrete) and the town is well surrounded by parks and gardens.

Of interest to walkers were the annual Falkirk Trysts, the largest cattle marts in the country. The scale was enormous: 60,000 cattle and 100,000 sheep are said to have been sold in one day. The drovers' routes, from the remotest Highlands, are one of our treasured legacies. The Highlands were thickly peopled then of course, but this does show a level of population and production that could be aimed for again, were the powers that be genuinely interested in the Highland economy, which stutters along on a feudal system of land ownership damaging to past history and future hopes. Beasts could not be fed in winter so the great trysts saw the surplus sold off. Many were walked on to the industrial cities of England, or even to Smithfield Market in London. The tryst was held to the south-east of Falkirk and later moved to Rough Castle and finally to Stenhousemuir, whose earlier name was Sheeplees.

The easiest way down to the town centre (or for Callendar Park/House) is just after coming out of the canal tunnel, which also gives access to Falkirk High railway station. From the station head down High Station Road which merges with the B8028 at a rather complex junction, overlooked by tower blocks. Turn up and first left (Kemper Ave) for Callendar Park/House. Heading down to town, after Comley Park primary school the road swings left, then as it swings right from a mini roundabout, go left, St Crispin's Place (becomes Cow Wynd) which leads to the pedestrianised High Street. There is no tourist office.

Despite being full of identikit multinationals, the centre has a lively air. Turn left towards the Steeple. The narrow lane before it is called Wooer Street; while other odd names are Bean Road, Ladysmill, Tanners Road and the Tattie Kirk. The Steeple dominates the High Street. This is actually the third Tolbooth Steeple. The original was rebuilt in 1697, but a century later the demolition of adjoining property so undermined the foundations it had to be taken down as well. For eleven years there was no Steeple, but funds were raised to build the present 140ft (43m) spire. The top section was rebuilt in 1927 after suffering a lightning strike. The weather cock went flying and masonry crashed everywhere, but the only fatality was a horse belonging to Mr (Irn-Bru) Barr. The Cross Well beside the Steeple dates to 1817, replacing one originally given to the town by the Livingstons of Callendar in 1681. The site of the Mercat Cross (and of the town's last public hanging in 1826) is marked out on the setts (rectangular cobbles). Tolbooth Street, behind the Steeple, makes the *Guinness Book of Records* as the shortest street in Britain.

Halfway along the High Street turn up through an arch to reach the solid old Faw Kirk (now Trinity Church) with its octagonal Adam tower, and, in the grounds, one of the oldest historical tombs in Scotland, that of a Graeme killed at the Battle of Falkirk in 1298. The church was rebuilt in 1771, and again in 1860 when the arched crown of Gothic ironwork was added, though the tower is earlier, and the site goes back to the start of historical time. The grounds were cleared of gravestones in 1962, except for

*The landmark
Falkirk steeple*

a few historical ones, like Sir John de Graeme's. There are tombs to victims of the 1746 Battle of Falkirk too: William Edmonstone and Munro of Foulis and his doctor brother. Foulis must have been a paragon; 'His death was universally regretted. Even by those who slew him'.

There are some impressive civic buildings; showing good Victorian confidence as so often. The Jacobean sheriff court was completed in 1868, but when the first Sheriff was appointed in 1834 everyone, perforce, had to use the ballroom of the Red Lion. The Carnegie Library is Gothic with some fine glass in the windows.

Walking out westwards, the Forth & Clyde Canal can be joined at Rosebank/Camelon (Lock 11), on the way passing, on the right, the attractive Dollar Park, named after Robert Dollar, who left it to the town. He was a Falkirk Bairn who emigrated to Canada and made a fortune. There are plenty of flowers and mature trees, and the large glasshouses produce nearly a quarter of a million bedding plants each year for use in the district. Beside the pavement stands the war memorial. A plaque for the First World War notes the horrific figure 'Over eleven hundred Falkirk Bairns died'.

The most interesting feature of Falkirk, for walkers especially, is Callendar Park and Callendar House, ten-minute walk east from the High Street. Aiming for it from Falkirk High Station has been mentioned; about 300 yards along the attractive Kemper Avenue there is a road into the magnificent Callendar Wood which can be circuited or, if Kemper Avenue is followed, there is a path off to the mansion once past the trees. Where to start? At Callendar House one can pick up leaflets on the many attractions.

Callendar House

Within the house there are exhibitions, a really excellent historical 'walk-through', a Historic Research Centre, and living experiences of a Georgian kitchen, the interpreters in period costume. You can glimpse the work of a clockmaker, printmaker and grocer too. One of the grand rooms is a tearoom. Walking straight out from the entrance of Callendar House, an ice house is passed before the road cuts through the very clear line of the *vallum* of the Antonine Wall. This bit of vandalism was done to make a grand entry for a visit from Queen Victoria; but her visit was cancelled. East of Callendar House a lime tree avenue leads to a large man-made loch (boating etc) while to the south lies an arboretum of mature trees and the slope of the great wood, offering endless explorations. The loch once fed a canal, which accounts for what looks like a ha-ha between house and woods. There's a range of amusements for children, and a pitch and putt course. However, the park-like setting, with the château-like mansion backed by the great wood, is in itself a delight. A place to visit often. Chapter 11 describes the Roman sites of the area, which offer attractive rural walking, then Chapter 12 continues the Forth and Clyde Canal description westwards, on to Auchinstarry.

The Forth & Clyde Canal

10

Kelpies
The Descent To The Forth
OSLR 65; OSE 349

The Wheel is the midpoint of the joint canals, with Bowling lying 32 miles west and Edinburgh 33 miles east. The Forth & Clyde towpath is joined over the small swing bridge. (How *big* the canal appears!) The south bank moorings are the base for many of the commercial canal boat hire companies. The *Marion Seagull* (2003) is the first Seagull Trust boat offering family/group accommodation, allowing disabled cruising (2–6 nights). A mile of walking east leads to Lock 16 and the Union Inn. The sprawl of Camelon (no Camelot, and pronounced Kam-lin) lies on the left with Tamfourhill on the far side. In 1973 a tar distillery in Tamfourhill went up in flames, and molten tar ran into the canal causing serious pollution.

The name Union Inn harks back to the canals in their prime, for this was where the Union Canal descended in a stairway of locks to unite with the Forth & Clyde Canal, at the large basin of Port Downie, busy with traffic. The basin and flight of locks were closed in 1933 and filled in thereafter. The Union Inn is still a welcome hostelry (with canal photographs on its walls), as is the Canal Inn by Lock 16, which lays claim to be the oldest canalside tavern on the Scottish canals.

In 1839 an experiment was carried out with canal boats towed by steam engines running along towpath tracks; a length of track was laid by Lock 16 and various weights of boat were moved, all very speedily and successfully. But applying the system throughout would have been prohibitively expensive, so the project was abandoned. (The Panama Canal would, however, see just such a scheme used.) Iron and chemical industries once existed here, and also a nail-making works. All had chimney stacks belching out smoke.

Lock 16 on the Forth & Clyde Canal by the Union Inn

A short walk from the Union Inn lies Watling Lodge with the finest section of the Roman *vallum*; well worth a visit, and described in Chapter 11.

Lock 16 has more crowded stagings. (I once saw a Dutch barge there.) There's a winding hole too. Right down to Lock 1 there are regular stagings and winding holes, so I'll generally not mention them again. One curiosity is seeing how the lock gate arms (lever lock balance beams) have the equivalent of kicking stones to give straining humans greater purchase.

Continuing, a road has to be crossed to follow Canal Street, a touch of surrounding suburbia with the park-like area off right, more or less on top of what was Port Downie. The Canal Inn is passed. Below Lock 15 is a display board explaining the three sculpted figures of a doctor, a swimming pool timekeeper, and the inventor of Iron Brew – local celebrities. (Barr's factory once occupied premises next to the Union Inn.) Lock 14 has a footbridge beside it.

The Rosebank Distillery buildings dominate Lock 11, with the Rosebank Beefeater restaurant/pub on the left. The remaining distillery buildings, with the chimney stack, lie across the busy road junction. The Beefeater is in the former bonded warehouse, and the interior is an impressive conversion and worth seeing. Both Lock 11 (and Lock 5) had to be repositioned in the work of restoration to fit in with road demands, and after the steep down and up under the Camelon road you can see the original lock, something of a narrow cutting now. Flats overlook the canal. There's an old lock-keeper's cottage at Lock 9, which drops the canal under a railway bridge (originally a swing bridge) so we are forced up and down steps to bypass the railway. Lock 8 leads into the Dollar Industrial Estate, and industry generally lines both banks down to Lock 4. Lock 5 lies by a busy road, with the Gambero Rosso Restaurant/Pizzeria prominent. Steps lead down to pass under the road (Bainsford Bridge) and the path rises to run along at a higher level than the usual towpath. There's a long straight length of canal to Lock 4 (Abbotshaugh) then a more rural continuation.

The A9 crosses the canal by a modern bridge, Orchardhall, painted blue. Over on the right now lies the vast Helix Park with its ponds and marshes, huge green sweeps, 17 miles of footpaths, the distant Falkirk football stadium, an outdoor stage, toilets and much else and, of course, culminating in the Kelpies, every bit as extraordinary as the Falkirk Wheel.

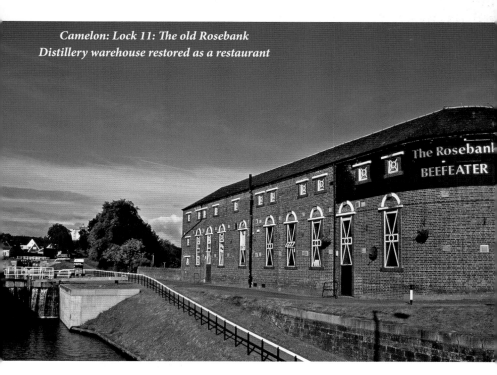

Camelon: Lock 11: The old Rosebank Distillery warehouse restored as a restaurant

There's a glimpse of them immediately after passing below the Orchardhall bridge.

Stagings mark a sharp left turn of the canal. When the canal was first created it ran straight on at this point to reach the sea at Grangemouth docks, but with all the developments (including the M9) restoring the route would have been impossible. The answer with the Millennium opening was to turn the canal here (Lock 3) and run on to a final lock, number 2, which was on the banks of the River Carron. This was tide-dependent and a Lock 1, on the river, was to be the hoped-for improvement, as and when possible. Instead we have the present continuation dominated by these two mythical beasts, one rearing 30m in to the air, the other bowing gracefully. They weigh in at 300 tonnes *each*. (Peer inside to see their construction.) In the sun they can glitter, but I've passed them on the M9 at gloomy dusk when they seemed quite menacing. The sculptor was Glaswegian Andy Scott, well known for his horse figure in Kelpie style on the M8 nearing Glasgow and the 10-metre tall four-armed female figure Arria off the M80 in Cumbernauld.

The Kelpies at sunset

The Wooden Spoon Seagull in Lock 3 near the Kelpies

After Lock 3 (crossing possible) still keep on the towpath side along past many moored boats (their names an interesting study!). There's a viewpoint up the bank giving one of the best views of the Kelpies. The towpath leads to another bend and the Carron Basin/Grangemouth or Kelpies Marina where there are residential moorings and all the facilities. The River Carron gate of old Lock 2 is now a dead end for the canal but can be crossed to reach land/water visitor facilities, shops and refreshments.

Halfway along this final canal stretch (moorings also along the other bank) there's a basin from which the canal enters Lock 2, which lies between the two Kelpies. To reach this means returning to Lock 3 for a crossing, or crossing the remains of old Lock 2 to the shopping and servicing area and further moorings. There's a Visitor Centre facing the Kelpies. Lock 2 (between the Kelpies) drops into a circular basin in something of a plaza, all very attractive – and very popular (in summer every car park is crowded with cars and buses).

From a pedestrian swing bridge by the Kelpies the canal heads below the roaring M9 (Edinburgh–Stirling road), and a final long straight lies ahead. There are several lengths of staging either side of the A905 Kerse Road Bridge (an operational lifting bridge) with the Saline Hills seen ahead,

From Lock 1, the sea lock to the Forth Estuary, looking to the Kelpies

a view dominated by the stumpy Longannet (Long-anat) power station chimney. The bigger range to the left is the Ochils. The canal runs parallel with the River Carron (left) while the town of Grangemouth lies to the right. After pipelines cross the River Carron, the final Lock 1 is reached, which is the link with the Firth of Forth. About turn! – and let us follow the great engineering feat of the Forth & Clyde Canal all the way up into the heart of Glasgow (20 locks) and on down to the sea again at Bowling on the Firth of Clyde (19 locks).

In the area surrounding the Kelpies you may have noticed brief one-line quotations. These are from a poem by Jim Carruth, and the whole poem is engraved on the platform by Lock 3:

Echo the great beasts that work among us
Unbridled in the Kingdom between canal and firth
Here to harness the river
Carry each weary traveller
Bow down your strong heads to taste the water
Stretch up your long necks to reach the sun.

Horses were the basic form of all transport during canal years, so it is right that they are remembered here. Additionally, in Scottish folklore a kelpie was a water spirit in horse form who would tempt the unwary onto his back with promises and then dash into the depths of a loch, the rider never to be seen again.

11

The Roman Wall:
Watling Lodge, Rough Castle, Seabegs Wood
OSLR 65; OSE 349

West of Camelon (Lock 16) and running on to Twechar (west of Kilsyth) are the best-preserved sections of the Antonine Wall which, running more or less parallel with the canal, offer side trips or excellent circular walks. Keeping these descriptions apart from those of the canal, Chapter 13 describes the sites over Croy Hill and Bar Hill; here, meanwhile, we have the Falkirk area's wall attractions, and then Chapter 12 follows the canal from the Falkirk Wheel on to Auchinstarry.

The Wall, this great Roman monument, deserves to be better known, though the feature has had a rough passage historically, with roads, railways, canals, buildings, industry and agriculture all wrecking its course across the waist of Scotland. Perhaps the worst damage was done in the 18th century. Before then, several of the sites had extensive ruins, and by the end of that century the 'convenient' stonework had been carried off to build houses, field walls, canal banks and much else. An interest in historical remains came a generation too late, World Heritage Site status more recently.

The Wall runs for 37 miles (60km), linking the River Forth near Bo'ness to the River Clyde at Old Kilpatrick, facing north, and generally commanding low ground, with forts at regular intervals along its length. Some, like Rough Castle and Bar Hill, are still of interest. The Wall was built of turf, though on a stone base, so it has not survived very well, nor has what could be called the service road which ran along behind the Wall, though this Military Way, as with Dere Street over the Cheviots, is often indicated by the pockmarkings of small quarries alongside.

The best surviving feature has been the *vallum*, or ditch, which ran along in front of the Wall – and the best lengths of that feature will be described. The main road heading out north beyond the Wall started at Camelon, just west of Falkirk, and there are traces of Roman forts and camps angling across behind the Ochils to Perth and up to the north-east of Scotland – far beyond Hadrian's Wall which tends to be regarded as the Romans' northern boundary. The boundary was seldom static in reality.

Caesar had first raided England in 55 BC and the real invasion began in AD 4. The governor Agricola first entered Scotland in AD 79, with the optimistic hope of adding it to the Roman Empire. Trimontium (Newstead) on the Tweed, named by the Romans for the triple-peaked Eildon Hills, became the main Borders base, and along the narrow waist of Scotland Agricola built a line of forts, quelled Galloway, and headed up to the north-east to win the great battle of Mons Graupius, the site of which remains tantalisingly unknown. His fleet reached as far as Orkney before he was recalled to Rome. Early the next century Rome withdrew from Scotland, back onto the Tyne–Solway line, and a decade later the Emperor Hadrian decided a definite defence line was needed, and commanded the building of the wall that bears his name.

His successor a decade later decided to re-invade Scotland, a project undertaken in AD 140 by the governor Urbicus – and so, a couple of years later, we had the Antonine Wall, which followed the line of Agricola's forts. Indeed, several of the new forts lie on top of the earlier defences. The Wall was held for a decade, then about AD 165, the Antonine Wall was finally abandoned for good. Three legions, about 8,000 men, were stationed on the Wall. Rome's waxing and waning fortunes led to their eventual departure from British shores, but that is another story. In this section, three sites within walking distance of the canal are described.

Watling Lodge (reached from Lock 16)

Watling Lodge offers one of the finest sections of Roman ditch on the Wall, still showing the deep V nature of this defensive feature. (Elsewhere the ditch is often much filled in and can be boggy.) With a wall on the south side of the ditch we can envisage just how formidable a barrier the Romans created. The soil dug out was always heaped up on the north side.

From the Union Inn (Lock 16) head off round the inn (away from the canal) and keep to the grass alongside the industrial building to reach Tamfourhill road. Cross at once to a gate with a Historic Scotland sign for Watling Lodge. Walk along the north bank of the *vallum*. All too soon this beech-lined ditch is interrupted: a brick building sits across it, one of the outbuildings of Watling Lodge. Sadly, the building appears to have been built on the main gateway/road through the Antonine Wall which led to Camelon, site of Roman forts and a Pictish town brutally levelled by Kenneth MacAlpin as he forged a single nation out of the Pictish and Scots

The vallum of the Roman Wall at Watling Lodge

tribes in the 840s. There are a few discontinuous sections of *vallum* beyond, but hardly worth exploring. Return to the Union Inn.

ROUGH CASTLE (REACHED FROM THE FALKIRK WHEEL)

This could be visited on coming out of the Rough Castle tunnel by taking a path up and over and round the canal exit to the far side, where the path to Rough Castle is signposted. Starting from the Falkirk Wheel, the path is signposted and rises to pass under the aqueduct – giving a different angle on that icon. Allow a couple of hours for the proposed circular walk to the fort and back.

Outward bound, keep to the well-made, well-signed path which wends along to community woodlands, much of it covering one-time mining areas. The path slowly loses height to near an abandoned bridge (with pipes) over the railway then climbs to soon reach the beautiful Rough Castle setting. (Antonine Wall sites are in the care of Historic Scotland). Keep along by the *vallum* to a display board by the northern entrance, then over right a bit to another board explaining a special feature.

This is the *lilia*, dug as a booby trap against mounted raiders. With sharpened stakes set in the bottom of the pits and their presence disguised, the pits would be a very effective way of breaking a charge. There is nothing much visible in the fort itself except vague shapes in the turf. The site was excavated in 1909, but then the foundations were covered over again to preserve them. Objects found during this excavation are in the Royal Museum of Scotland, Edinburgh, where they are, with other Roman remains, given a room to themselves, and make a fascinating display.

The western entrance has subtle defences and there's a fine view of the *vallum* as it runs down and up the hollow of the Rowan Tree Burn and on westwards.

Leave the attractive site from the eastern entrance and take the exit signposted for the Falkirk Wheel and Tamfourhill to wander through woodland then out to meadowlands where birch and willow are growing apace. The woodland edge is followed to a gravel path and, at a fork, left is signed for the Wheel and soon rejoins the outward route. Whichever option is taken, it is worth going over the top of the tunnel exit for the view it gives of the aqueduct/wheel and the spread of country with the Ochils dominant.

The booby trap of the lilia at Rough Castle

In the days of cattle droving, Rough Castle was for one period the site of the Falkirk Tryst, which had started near Polmont after overtaking Crieff as the main market. About 1785, possibly because the new Forth & Clyde Canal made access difficult, it finally moved to Stenhousemuir. The coming of the railways and changes in agricultural methods saw droving largely die out in the1860s.

SEABEGS WOOD (REACHED BY UNDERPASS OR B816)

This site is reached by a curious pedestrian underpass a kilometre or so west of Bonnybridge. Car drivers can reach it from Bonnybridge (east) or Castlecary (west) along the B816, but there is scant parking space, and the towpath approach is the safest.

Seabegs Wood, an oak wood, has been well tidied and gives another good idea of the frontier line. The military road has its best-preserved length here, the wall line is obvious and the upthrown ditch material makes quite a rampart. There is an interpretive board (Historic Scotland); altogether a pleasant spot. But how history can turn on little accidents: Robert the Bruce was nearly killed when hunting here in 1300 when he was attacked by a wild white bull.

12

Falkirk Wheel to Auchinstarry
OSLR 65, 64; OSE 349

There's plenty of staging for boats as we leave the Falkirk Wheel site. A double railway line is crossed and a track leads down to parking and 'park and ride' facilities. The railway came 70 years after the canal, so burrowing below the canal was a major undertaking. We are soon back to rural walking, with a birch wood across the water on what was mining dereliction, and fields to the right. Pylon lines cross to a sub-station to the north; just before the first a burn flows under which has the yellowy colour of old mine workings, by the second there is an overspill. Most people are struck by the size of the canal here if they have only experienced the Union Canal; the Forth & Clyde appears huge, but it was designed to take seagoing vessels. After an open stretch there are fine trees on the left as the outskirts of Bonnybridge are reached. Several houses have created a brilliant stretch of garden beside the towpath (see page 81).

We swing round Cowden Hill (the trig only 59 metres but a good viewpoint) to reach one of the canal's lifting bridges (hence the traffic lights) which was opened in 2002. Nearing the bridge there is one of the Forth and Clyde Canal oval distance markers: 'Underwood Lock, 2 km, Falkirk 6½ km'. We'll see others as we go along, some with this misuse of decimals. Bonnybridge has shops just down the brae, then off left, but another feature that few books mention is a *must* for seeing. Head down the brae and turn right at a garage. You will see a small tunnel with another yellowy stream flowing out of it. There is a raised walkway through this pend, which gave workers access before the road bridge was built over the canal. It is worth going through after reading the note on the arch: 'The Radical Pend. Named to commemorate the Battle of Bonnymuir. April 5th 1820'. Depression years and hard working conditions in the post-Napoleonic years gave rise to demands for universal suffrage, parliamentary reform etc. Demonstrations were suppressed violently, as in the 1819 Peterloo Massacre in Manchester. Here, a group of 300 Calton (Glasgow) weavers got caught up in a march

The Radical Pend, Bonnybridge

to Falkirk and were met by mounted troops, who soon dispersed the crowd. Battle it was not, but three were executed for sedition and others transported. Hard to envisage Bonnybridge as a sprawl of industrial works, the last of which only vanished in my lifetime. A more recent claim to fame is that Bonnybridge has had more lottery winners than any other place in the country.

Once through the pend, turn right up a small lane to walk round the brick houses (Hunter Gardens) and so back to the canal. Continuing, Bonnybridge sprawls on, on the south side while below, north, flows the Bonny Water. This rises south-east of Cumbernauld, bisects that town as the Vault Glen, and passes under the canal just west of the A80 before continuing parallel to the canal (to the north) and finally joining the River Carron north-east of Bonnybridge.

Our third Roman site, Seabegs Wood, is another short diversion, reached by a pedestrian underpass, the pend being another right of way for miners going to work, which the canal builders had to respect. Look out for a footpath running along below the towpath and where it comes up to the towpath head down, turn left, and there is the pend. On the other side of the canal steps, right, lead to the site.

The C19 ironworks by the canal at Bonnybridge

Towpath gardens, by Bonnybridge

Back on the towpath, another kilometre leads to Lock 17. (Lock 16 feels a long way back.) The canal's stable building here had been turned into a restaurant but sadly is now a burnt-out wreck. There's a footbridge over to a car park by the B816. If not noticed already, in high summer the Forth & Clyde Canal abounds with yellow waterlilies. Continuing, it feels wooded, but this, as with roads and railways, is only a thin edging which (in some places) could do with cutting to allow views. On to Glasgow, we now have the Kilsyth/Campsie Fells in sight.

Locks 18 and 19, the former with a lock-keeper's cottage, give a pause before the thundering M80 ahead. In front of the M80 there's an MM-style bridge which leads a very minor road across for the benefit of just one household! (At one time it was a swing bridge and a more important road.) The bascule bridge Forth & Clyde Canal logo is on the parapet. A large MM then marks the brutally practical M80 Castlecary Bridge. The then A80 had completely blocked the canal in 1963, an event that was something of a death blow to the decaying canal.

Castlecary occupies one of those places where geography influences history: Roman road and wall, canal, railway and modern roads culminating in the M80 all crisscross in a bewildering array at Castlecary. The auxiliary Roman fort was one of the few built of stone, and excavations yielded many coins, weapons, urns and other items, and also an altar ingratiatingly dedicated to the god Mercury by the Sixth Legion. Castle, roads and railway have largely demolished the site. The sturdy keep that gave the village its name was the seat of the Baillie family, descendants of the Balliols. The Jacobites burned the castle in 1715, but it has been restored as a private house.

Arrowhead, *Sagittaria sagittifolia*, is a plant thriving in the canal here, and in several places back to and in the Union Canal, yet it is not supposed to grow north of the Tyne. The plant will only grow in unpolluted waters, which is something to commend the canal.

Just past the M80 there's a path off: 'Hazel Road, Banknock'. Railings (on parapet foundations) mark where the Red Burn passes under the canal, shortly to be joined by the Bonny Water, which has all the time been wending east as we've been heading west. A distillery once lay beside the canal as we come to Wyndford (Banknock) Lock 20, which is important as the eastern lock of the summit pound (stretch) of the Forth & Clyde Canal. It has taken a dozen miles from the Forth to reach this summit. The western end of this summit level is in Glasgow! The Bonny is still below, on the right, and rises in the hills to the north, as do waters joining the infant

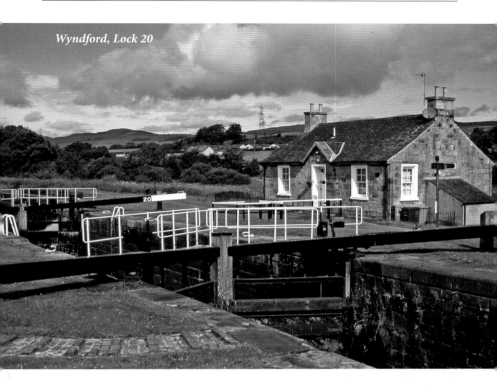

Wyndford, Lock 20

Kelvin. The watershed between Forth and Clyde lies somewhere along the next reach of canal – an infamous reach historically.

Lock-keeper's cottage and stables (now a house) have survived at Wyndford Lock (pronounced Wined-ford). Walking on, narrows mark an abandoned stop lock, then there's a spillway, where you can see how a stop lock worked on the canal. We next come on a unique feature: the canal becomes much wider for a couple of miles. This is the stretch of the notorious Dullatur Bog, which the confident builders decided to cross in a straight line. The bog had to be drained as much as could be (its waters created the infant River Kelvin), then a huge embankment created. This was sunk 50m (164ft) into the bog before it stabilised! Then they could build the canal: the north side and towpath carefully established and the water simply finding its own level on the south side, hence the greater, and variable width. One sensational event marked the work in the Dullatur (Dollater) Bog: a mass exodus of frogs, tens of thousands of them, which swarmed over the countryside to the dismay of everyone. The local minister was not slow to produce sermons drawing Biblical comparisons.

Dullatur Bog is a SWT reserve. Wildlife treats the whole canal as an elongated loch, but one with a shoreline out of all proportion to the area of water. Perhaps elongated river would be more accurate, for the canal 'flows'; it is not static water. The flow is controlled so that spates don't tear away riverside vegetation, or droughts reduce the banks to smelly disaster. The canal is a unique environment, and its wildlife features will become comfortably familiar to towpath wanderers. Top of the predation chain would appear to be man, as fisherman. Pike, another voracious predator, may be seen lurking by the edge of the reeds. They will take ducklings as well as smaller fish, even other pike. Fish weighing 20lb/9kg have been caught. Perch and roach are also long established, and tench and bream have been introduced. In the Dullatur Bog, a dead trooper, among other casualties, was found still sitting in the saddle of the horse on which he had fled from the Battle of Kilsyth. The bog had engulfed them. Baillie, the Covenanting general, nearly came to grief in the bog too, but struggled through to Castle Cary, then owned by a cousin.

Witchcraft and superstition lingered long in this area; into the 19th century there were known 'witches'. A sceptical farmer met one when

On the Dullatur
  Bog reach

carting along the canal bank and gave her a piece of his mind. She held up her fingers and muttered a curse before taking to the fields. The farmer laughed and plodded on. The sedate mare, however, suddenly went daft and plunged, cart, farmer and all, into the canal. (One suspects the farmer had to have some excuse.)

There's a small basin cut into the south bank at one spot and staging at another and from the towpath a path is signed for Kelvinhead and Banton. Power lines (pylons obvious) end the long Dullatur Bog straight, and an unusually big basin marks the site of Craigmarloch which, in the glory days of canal boat trips (*Fairy Queen, May Queen, Gipsy Queen*), had a restaurant, *The Bungalow*, a putting green and other tourist attractions. Hard to imagine now.

Round the bend there's the steeply angled Craigmarloch/Dullatur Bridge, which replaced an original bascule bridge and a car park and picnic tables, display board, etc. One feature is a feeder for the Forth & Clyde Canal running into the canal. (A lock spills 80,000 gallons of water every time it is used, so topping up is essential.) The feeder comes down from Banton (Townhead) Loch, a reservoir which taps the Birkenburn Reservoir and Garrel Burn which come off the Kilsyth Hills. This feeder circles a hill, passes the canal stable ruins and enters here. Looking up the feeder, the old stable block can be glimpsed, a ruin, bricked up and abandoned. It sits so far from the towpath because an earlier, closer, building just sank into the boggy ground. A quarry behind the stable supplied stone for constructing the canal. The battle symbol and date 1645 *on* Banton Reservoir looks odd, but the battle predated reservoir or canal. More about the battle later, but names like Baggage Knowe and Slaughter Howe are other geographic references to it.

Just west of the bridge is an overflow from the canal, the canal being higher than the infant River Kelvin and the large alluvial plain stretching over towards Kilsyth. There's a small boat staging. Here too there are options of walking with some, perhaps quite welcome, up-hills to see the most interesting sections of the Antonine Wall in a setting more usually associated with such structures. They could be followed as westering alternatives to the towpath, or made into circular walks. They are fine viewpoints, as akin to those on Hadrian's Wall as Antoninus could manage. They are described in the next chapter, 13, then Chapter 14 briefly looks at Kilsyth before Chapter 15 takes the canal on into the heart of Glasgow.

From Craigmarloch the canal runs along under wooded Croy Hill with many a wiggle, then there is a pleasant stretch on to Auchinstarry with long staging leading to a big basin, which is a major marina with all the facilities of

Nearing Craigmarloch

such, the largest on our two canals. Scottish Canals have an office overlooking the site, there's bike and canoe hiring, the Port Gallery, and the Boathouse, with bar, restaurant and offering 'boutique rooms'. A circular walk runs along the south side of the canal then circles Nethercroy Woodland, returning via an old whinstone quarry and ponds (allow 1 hour). There's also a 'sensory garden' above the parking area, at the top end of which is a striking ceramic 'mini totem pole' about the Forth & Clyde Canal history and a ceramic map of the area. The eye is drawn to a large whinstone quarry, the cliffs overlooking a deep pond, used for fishing instruction, as the cliffs are for climbing. Picnic tables allow grandstand observation. I once saw an advert for a lecture by a famous climber, entitled 'World Rock', which would cover 'Australia, Yosemite, Italy, France and Auchinstarry Quarry'.

Auchinstarry Marina

Auchinstarry (Auchinsterrie) was where Kilsyth coal would be loaded onto canal boats to take it to Glasgow and even to Belfast. Later, the mineral lines all converged on Twechar, and then railways completely took over from the canal. Auchinstarry quarry produced the whinstone 'setts' that paved the streets of Glasgow, and dates back to the 18th century. Kilsyth lies north of Auchinstarry Bridge; to the west is the wetland bird reserve of Dumbreck Marsh. The Auchinstarry Bridge is another built to slope upwards, replacing a swing bridge, the abutments of which lie west of the new bridge, on the original road line.

Before continuing, do read Chapter 14 and at least walk the five minutes to the graveyard to see the Kilsyth family vault with its weird history (see page 97-99).

13

The Roman Wall:
Croy Hill and Bar Hill
OSLR 64; OSE 349

With this hilly ground available to them, the Romans, unsurprisingly, ran their defence line along the crest of the hills. Until comparatively recent times, low ground across Scotland's central belt was boggy in many places, one reason the canal was such a boon to travel: compare its ease to a coach 'plaistering through the glaur' as was the usual inter-city travellers' complaint. Croy Hill and Bar Hill can be done separately or together as pleasant circular walks in conjunction with the canal.

Start at Craigmarloch Bridge and walk up the Dullatur–Cumbernauld road. About 70m on, go right through gates to start the traverse of Croy Hill. The route is well signposted and there are Antonine Wall and John Muir Way marker discs throughout. Steep zigzags gain the initial height. There are picnic tables and a view down to the Craigmarloch basin – once buzzing with its tearoom and trippers!

The railway will probably be heard if not seen – your last contact with this inter-city artery which passes south of Croy Hill in a deep, 1.5km cutting. An alternative line, the Kelvin Valley Railway, wound along by the hills to the north, linked with the Kilsyth and Bonnybridge line at Kilsyth. John Thomas's *Forgotten Railways* has some interesting stories. Coal mining – on Croy Hill and Bar Hill, at Twechar, Shirva, St Flannan, Tintock, Cadder, all on or near the canal – has vanished with almost no trace. There's still an active quarry along the south flank of Croy Hill.

The path winds on, up towards a clump of trees which mark the site of a Roman fort, (or you can follow the deep V of the ditch). Just before the sycamore clump there is no ditch, the rock being too hard even for the Roman soldiers to work. The main path arcs left and then right to gain the northern scarp, a good defence in itself. The *vallum* is overgrown but can be traced. Croy Hill is a fine viewpoint, with the crowded Auchinstarry marina, quarry and sprawl of Kilsyth all clear. Keep along and down the scarp. Croy suddenly comes into view. From the kissing gate exit, the *vallum* back up is clear, hewn out of rock.

You come out onto a tarred road, and when this soon swings left, turn right (gate, signposts). After passing a transformer, leave the road, left. An abandoned quarry is on the right. At the next signpost, turn off left along a grass track to a gate where the B802 is crossed. (The track on, and another track on the other side of the B802, descend to Auchinstarry and the marina.)

A sign for Bar Hill indicates the track across the road. Take this farm track (which runs up along the Roman line), ignoring left forks, on to a gate leading into a cool deciduous wood. Ignore paths leading off to the left. When an open green space is reached (the green swathe, straight on up the forest ride, is the line of the Military Way), bear right. (Forestry Commission/John Muir signs.) On a rise there's an explanation board by Historic Scotland about Bar Hill in the Roman period. (They spell it Bar, but others have Barr.) And what a view of our route: no Roman concessions to topography. The ground falls away then rises steeply, and the easiest

The Roman vallum descending from Castle Hill

walking is by the forest edge. At the top end of the wood a final pull up a cone of hill lands the walker at the prominent trig point of Castle Hill (155m/508ft), the highest part of Bar Hill (and of the whole defensive system) and, naturally, a superb viewpoint. On a clear day both Forth and Clyde waters can be seen, and the hills to the north are spread in fine array beyond the ever-expanding sprawl of Kilsyth. (The summit has traces of an Iron Age fort.)

Wend on through open woodland, left rather than straight ahead, to arrive on top of Bar Hill, where the outline of the Roman fort has been preserved. The setting is splendid, with the view to the Campsies running westwards to the dip of the Blane and then on to the Kilpatrick Hills, and with the spread of Cumbernauld and Glasgow a contrast to the south. The site is well explained. When the Romans departed, all manner of things were thrown down to choke the well (a treasure trove for archaeologists) including the winding gear of the well itself, an altar, weapons, tools, ballista balls, over 20 columns, bases and capitals from the headquarters building, pottery and much else, all preserved till dug out in the 20th century. (Some finds are in the museum at Kirkintilloch, others in Edinburgh.) Bar Hill Fort is unusual in being sited back from the wall, so the Military Way passes between fort and wall/ditch.

Another notice board, down to the right (north-west), explains the ruins of the separate bath-house and latrines. Every fort had its bath-house, laid out in roughly similar fashion. You entered a changing room, then a cold wash room before a series of ever-hotter bathrooms. The heat came from under-floor and/or inter-wall ducts, the air being heated in a furnace at the end of the building. The toilet block would usually be sited downhill slightly, so waste water could be channelled down to flush it. A trip to the toilet was a sociable event – the room was fitted with the optimum number of wooden seats ranged round the walls and lined over troughs. All very hygienic and organised, very Roman. One find here was a rubbish pit with things like broken pottery and old boots – and eleven human hand and foot bones.

Continue from the fort, descending towards the south-west to a gate with the round dome of a water tank very visible. A second gate exits onto a farm track. Turn right to follow this down to Twechar, coming to the main road beside the war memorial, then walk down the road to the canal. The houses passed were those of the staff of the coal mines, the teacher, minister and such. The miners' rows have long been demolished and new areas of housing created further west.

*Roman bathhouse remains
at the Bar Hill fort*

14

Historic Kilsyth
OSLR 64; OSE 349 or 348

Following the B802 from Auchinstarry into Kilsyth, you see the town sign bearing the burgh's coat of arms, and just beyond, left, is the pepperpot watch-house in the cemetery. Under this watch-house lies the Kilsyth family vault, of which a gruesome story will be told on our return walk.

The road into Kilsyth dips, then pulls up again. Cross it, to note the monument erected to the memory of a minister who died in 1910; apparently Mr Jeffrey 'wore the White Flower of a blameless life'. Kilsyth has a tradition of religious fervour dating back to Covenanting times, which became most notable during religious revivals in the mid-18th and 19th centuries. Few towns have as many churches. Keep on the same side up to a decoratively planted roundabout, cross at once, and head down a pedestrian path which leads through an arch (pend) into the heart of the town, a few steps taking the architecture back a century.

Turn right at once along Market Street to an attractive square with an 1869 fountain and continue, then turn left onto Burngreen, laid out as a park in 1910. The bridges over the various streams have fine period railings as, for safety, they could not be removed during World War II. The war memorial has a truly shockingly long list of names on it. There is a bandstand in the centre of the park and a painted lady fountain (both cast by Kirkintilloch's Lion Foundry). I've also seen the lady in Kirki, and in Tomintoul. The attractive library at the end of the park, right, has an upstairs room with historical displays and information. Further on there is another park for sport, but head back across Burngreen to exit by a modern-style bridge where the Garrel and Ebroch burns meet.

Ahead, there's another bridge with fine old, circular cast iron decoration from which you see the monument to the once-important mining industry. (Something like 4,000 miners lost their jobs locally in the second half of the 20th century.) Kilsyth even had two railway stations. From the monument follow a footpath by the burn (more good railings) to come on a circular

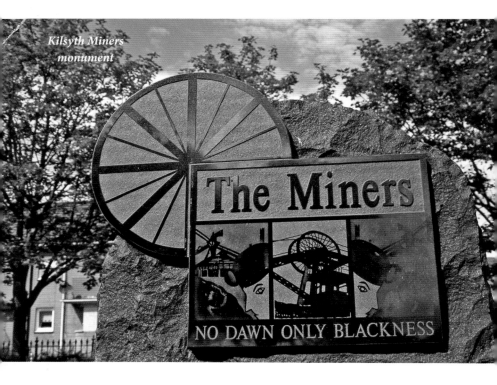

Kilsyth Miners monument

stone (seat round it) inscribed 'and search for minnows in the burn till come the time to home return'. Left is the pedestrianised Main Street, ahead more shops, right, Post Office and café. Kilsyth has become a vast sprawl of modern houses yet Main Street has a village air.

Some historical notes of interest before returning to the canal. The 1645 battle symbol was noted earlier on Banton reservoir, the canal feeder; that battle was the last of Montrose's victories in his *annus mirabilis*. While Montrose was in north-east Scotland, Cromwell had inflicted a crushing defeat on the King's forces at Naseby, and Montrose realised that however many Covenanting armies he defeated in the north, the result would be marginal. He had to move south. In the middle of August the two opposing forces found themselves face to face at Kilsyth.

The Covenanters' general, Baillie, had the larger force, but was hampered by his serving a committee which included the Earls of Argyll, Elcho, Burleigh and Balcarres, who had all suffered under Montrose's Highlanders and could not agree on tactics. Montrose was encamped below the Campsies, the Covenanters were on a ridge above. Quite why

Montrose had allowed his opponents the higher ground is not known, but the ground between was not suitable for cavalry and Baillie was wary about a possible trap. His committee, however, felt they had caught Montrose at last, and to leave him no chance of escape they began to shift their men across Montrose's front to occupy a dominant hill from which they would swoop down.

In a glen below their route, a small force of MacLeans occupied some houses, and a small body from the Covenanters' column broke off to attack them, but were repulsed and chased back. This was too much for some clansmen, who charged after them; sweeping through the column and before long, the Covenanting army was in full flight. Scotland belonged to Montrose, the King's Captain General. But south of the border there was no Montrose, and his defeat at Philiphaugh near Selkirk was only a month away. He was to lose his wife and eldest son the same year. He was only 38 when he was executed. Five years after the Battle of Kilsyth, Cromwell marched into Scotland and, following his 'crowning mercy' of victory at the Battle of Dunbar, carried on into the west. On the way he blew up the Livingston castle at Kilsyth.

The *Statistical Account* is very thorough on Kilsyth, and full of fascinating descriptions of work generally, and particular topics like the creation of a cut to take the River Kelvin, or the coming of the canal. The minister describes the local climate as 'rather watery'. In 1733 the area was hit by a freak thunderstorm when three-inch hailstones wrought havoc and left the country under water. The burns came down off the hills in torrents and did a great deal of damage (20-ton boulders were trundled down) but, amazingly, no human life was lost. A woman and child had a fright when a bolt of lightning came down the chimney as they sat close to the fire and killed the unfortunate cat at their feet.

East of Kilsyth is the Colzium Lennox Estate (park) and its mansion, which was given to the town in 1937. A plinth below the house commemorates the battle, but boobs in ascribing the victory to the Duke (*sic*) of Montrose. (The Grahams only gained that title through supporting the 1707 Union sell-out, and the local Livingston, Lord Kilsyth, fought its every clause.) The grounds are immaculately kept and full of interesting shrubs and trees, ablaze in autumn colours. The walled garden is a 'glorious gem'. The old laundry has been restored and turned into the Clock Theatre, named after the clock above it, which dates from 1863. Just up from the bridge, leading to the house, is a well-preserved example of an ice house. Townhead (Banton) Reservoir lies just below and to the east, and is the

In the walled garden, Colzium Lennox Estate

main feeder for the Forth & Clyde Canal. (The Garrel Burn coming off the Campsies was tapped to feed the reservoir (1773) and runs across the park as a lade, even crossing over another burn.)

Follow round the south side of the reservoir, a Smeaton creation and, at the time, the largest such in Scotland. Paths are signed for Banton. There's a big concrete reservoir overflow and the start of the feeder below. Sadly this can't be followed to the Forth & Clyde Canal. A popular local walk continues to the hamlet of Banton then crosses the A803 at Kelvinhead to join a path down to the canal on the Dullatur Bog reach – and so back to Kilsyth. From the town centre Colzium can best be reached afoot by the Pat McCann Walkway which comes out opposite the park gates. A path also comes down to here from the Banton/Townhead reservoir, allowing a shorter circular walk.

From Burngreen, cross a footbridge opposite the bandstand (south side) and follow the burn up, cross it, pass a football pitch, then a road off the A803, before a long stretch behind houses (once a railway) to come out opposite the estate entrance. This spot can also be reached from the Auchinstarry Quarry car park, opening up another circuit: up via the old Coach Road and back by the McCann. The start is signposted. At a fork keep right, to eventually come out on a tarred road. Turn right (Coach Road) and walk on past houses for c. 200m to where a sign, left, points to a gentle rising path (the Avenue) up to the A803.

Patrick McCann was a popular provost of the town; there's a plaque to him on the railings near the Mining Monument. And along a bit, a bust to another provost, John Jarvie, who has a square named after him. The mining monument was designed and constructed by pupils from the two local academies.

In 1739, the Colzium estate factor was responsible for introducing the potato to Scotland. Robert Graham began experimenting with potatoes in his garden near Banton and planted out crops above Kilsyth. An astute businessman, he bought up farms right across Scotland and planted potatoes. As they say, the rest is history. But back to the canal.

Just before taking the pend out from Main Street, note another stone/seat on the right, this inscribed 'waters of the Garrel flow by blacken slopes', (these words from local poet William Bell). Head off down the busy Auchinstarry road and cross, to go into the graveyard. On entering, note the unusual lamb sculptures on stones to left and right, memorials to young girls and a change from the ubiquitous draped urn, which is even present on a cast iron 'stone'. There are also several interesting older stones (some lying flat), obviously the work of one mason, filled with symbols: trumpet, open book, hourglass, shuttle, a ship under sail and topped by a winged spirit with angular wings. But the main fascination is the Kilsyth mausoleum: quite a story.

The Livingston support for the Stewarts was to have a somewhat macabre outcome. The ill-fated Bonnie Dundee, who died in his moment of victory at the Battle of Killiecrankie (1689), had married Jean Cochrane, granddaughter of the Earl of Dundonald, who then, as his widow, married William Livingston (later Viscount Kilsyth) with whom she went into exile. On a visit to Rotterdam in 1695, the couple were making a goodnight visit to their infant, asleep with her nurse, when the roof fell in and all but Livingston were killed. The bodies were embalmed and brought home to Kilsyth. In 1795 the vault was accidentally opened by some students who had forced a way in and the bodies were found to be remarkably well preserved, as if just newly interred. They became something of a spectacle before the vault was closed again. I found this in a book dated 1872 and

*The Kilsyth Mausoleum
(and watch house)*

visited the site in 1989, a year when another, official, inspection showed the bodies were still preserved – 300 years on.

It was at Colzium that the widowed Jean met and fell in love with Lord Kilsyth and exchanged gold rings in the garden. She soon managed to lose hers (dreadful omen!) and then so did he – but, remarkably, both were found many years later when new owners were altering the layout of the garden.

15

Auchinstarry To Kirkintilloch
OSLR 64; OSE 348, 342

Setting off from Auchinstarry, Glasgow is 22km and Falkirk 17km. The fine curve of stonework is for the original swing bridge. The canal wends below Castle Hill/Bar Hill on a high embankment, with some re-inforcing on the tightest bends where boats might hit the bank. All signs of the once extensive mines and quarries have disappeared in the spread of trees. Yellow lilies are almost continuous now – but keep an eye open for the rarer white ones. We are soon walking along above the B8023, Kil-syth still a sprawl visible below the Campsies and Queenzieburn west of it. Eventually the towpath and road are merely separated by a railing, and for the last 70 metres to the Twechar Bridge there is a thin strip of pave-ment. On the far side there is staging and a slip. The Twechar Bridge is a lifting bridge, and alongside it are the abutments of an earlier swing bridge.

Twechar is almost unpronounce-able unless you were born there; try *twek-ar* (the 1823 *Companion* had *Quecher*). It never starts by rhyming with *wheech*. Created as a mining village in 1860, the original miners' rows have gone, and housing schemes sprawl westwards. The school and church and better old buildings lie up the road south, where walkers descending from Bar Hill Roman fort exit. The map is littered with

The canal between Kilsyth and Twechar

The Twechar lifting bridge

'Quarry (*dis*)' indications. The last pit in the area closed in 1968. The canal had at one period been bridged west of Twechar Bridge to link pits on the condition coal was moved by barges, a deal which was honoured long after all other pits had turned to railways.

There are two options for continuing: to keep along the towpath for a stretch still tight against the B8023, until the road is forced away by Shirva Farm (the towpath is backed by gabions as it swings left to pass the farm); and the alternative, recommended, is to walk the south side of the canal as far as Shirva Farm. (The canal here lies on the Roman wall line.) Walk along the road parallel to the canal, passing a village store, then continue on a track which runs along the backs of houses, with sheds and garages. At the last house, descend steeply on paths to the Broad Burn. Don't cross the bridge, but head through the pend and the steps up to the towpath. There is a date 1771 above the arch at the north end. Just before the pend, right, is a distinct piece of Roman *vallum*, the last Antonine Wall bit of ditch we will see. (From that bridge over the Broad Burn a path runs on the south of the canal through to Kirkintilloch.)

Continuing, there is another canal stable block, now a fenced-off, dangerous ruin. An overspill follows. Puzzling is what looks like a Union Canal milestone but with the letters FCN inscribed. (Forth & Clyde Navigation; probably a boundary stone originally.)

The hamlet of Tintock lies hidden across the canal, originally a scattered weavers' base in a lonely setting, later with several pits nearby, one with a mineral line to the canal. There is a staging by a couple of houses, an attractive spot. Look out for a path sloping back down from the towpath. This leads to the Tintock pend arch with its low headroom of 4'9" (1.3m), still used by cars, rather like the Radical Pend.

At a bend a path angles down to the junction of the B8023 with the A803 Kilsyth road which crosses the still small River Kelvin. The Kelvin flows on to skirt the north of Kirkintilloch, adding the Glazert Water which drains the western Campsies and the Luggie Water flowing from Cumbernauld – and then, as a contorted big flow on a flood plain, giving marvellous examples of oxbow lakes. 'The Kelvin comes to Kirki a dribble and leaves as a flow'. A pipe is bridged over the canal. On the south side is the bold brick St Flannan's Roman Catholic church, well worth a visit as it is only five minutes' walk from Hillhead Bridge, and the airy, dramatic, modern interior is beautiful.

We finally come on the 1938 Hillhead swing bridge (replacing an original bascule bridge) with its ironwork and lantern finials, stagings and a basin. The canal's greater width goes back to Kirki's days as Scotland's first inland port (1773). Herring might be sold off boats which came through from the Forth (5p a pailful), there were timber yards, and a thriving import/export business, besides local foundries and mines. The town would have had mixed feelings when the canal was cut westwards to Glasgow.

Fine railings draw attention to a notable engineering feature, the huge single arch over the Luggie Water, but note how a railway once went under the arch. This Campsie Branch Railway was added in the 1840s, which hardly detracts from the massive yet graceful arch – well worth going down to see.

A concrete flyover (Nicholson Bridge) follows, stark on its round pillars, noisy with 'doos', and the canal busy with ducks and swans who receive handouts galore. The next landmark, St Mary's (red stone) parish church, was built in 1914 to replace the Auld Kirk, which is now the excellent museum. The Cowgate (the town's main street) crosses the Townhead Bridge. The original bascule bridge had been replaced in the 1930s with a swing bridge, and then the canal was culverted in the destructive Sixties. The present plain concrete bridge rests on the old abutments. The building over on the corner of the Cowgate was the Eagle Inn, where the owner, Sandy Taylor, supplied horses for towing during the 19th century, and operated passenger boats.

Kirkintilloch is more or less in the middle of the long summit pound. In 1836 about a quarter of a million passengers were carried city to city, commercial craft passed constantly, even the herring fleet might hurry through from Clyde to Forth in pursuit of the 'silver darlings'. The bridge area has been attractively landscaped. By turning right down the Cowgate you can find most of the town's services. The next chapter takes the canal on from Kirki right into the heart of Glasgow, but a bit about the town first.

Kirkintilloch's name, anciently, was Caerpentaloch, the fort at the head of the ridge. Note the 1893 fountain with the motto over it: Ca' canny but ca' awa' ('Be careful but carry on'). The centre is modern but has some character; walk to the Cross at the far end to visit the Auld Kirk (1644) Museum containing award-winning displays on the town's major past industries: coal mining, iron works, shipbuilding and weaving. The Lion Foundry made the red telephone boxes which were known all over the world, now sadly phased out and the works forced to close as a result.

The Barony Chambers next door dates to 1815, when it replaced the old tollbooth. The top floor had a school, the middle floor acted as town hall and court room, and below lay the gaol. The steeple's clock was known as the 'four-faced liar', as each face tended to show a different time. The museum can supply a leaflet/map of the Peel Park.

Behind the Auld Kirk are war memorial gates leading into Peel Park, where there is a fountain and bandstand (as at Kilsyth), a good view to the Campsies, an excavated section of Wall foundation and the site of a castle motte. Walk down the park left to Union Street and then left back to the Cowgate. There's another red church (St Ninian's Roman Catholic) beside Peel Park. Kirkintilloch, like Kilsyth, has plenty of churches, sharing the same history of religious revivals in the 18th and 19th centuries. South of the canal lies Townhead; the only interest there is a couple of pubs/restaurants.

Kirkintilloch developed as a result of the canal coming. There were two shipyards, and industries developed as they could use the canal for transport; Glasgow was able to trade with eastern Europe via the canal. Maryhill (Kelvinlock then) had the first registered Temperance Society in 1827, and Kirkintilloch was also a dry town for 47 years, between 1921 and 1968. Records still show that many of the accidents on the canal had alcohol to blame – drunk in charge of a scow, screw or gabbart perhaps! Something like three million tons of goods and 200,000 passengers were being carried annually in mid-Victorian times.

The Fairy Queen
at Kirkintilloch

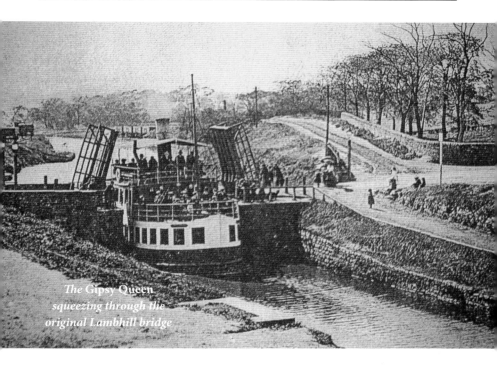

The Gipsy Queen squeezing through the original Lambhill bridge

From late Victorian times until World War II, cruising on the canal was popular (an alternative to sailing 'doon the watter'). The famous '*Queens*' regularly ran to the basin at Craigmarloch (Kilsyth) with its tearoom and putting green. A band and singing enlivened the evening run home to Glasgow. This is the image which lingers, rather than the reality of the canals being for 200 years as vital for industrial transportation as are the motorways today.

Robert the Bruce gave Kirkintilloch's castle and lands to the Flemings, but they rebuilt the castle at Cumbernauld as their base. Edward I seized the castle at Kirkintilloch, but Bishop Wishart paused in his building work on Glasgow Cathedral to help dislodge the English forces. Bonnie Prince Charlie's army passed through Kirkintilloch on the way to the Battle of Falkirk. A shot was fired after the troops, who had to be placated to stop them sacking the town. The library has a treasured burgh 'Court Book' (1658–94) which contains a range of historical information. In those days it was a crime in Kirki to be unemployed.

Kirkintilloch was early involved in railways as well as canals, a line being built from the mines at Monkland in 1826 (for horse-drawn wagons) to take coal by the canal to Edinburgh. Lines proliferated, and in 1840 another went by Slamannan to the Union Canal at Causewayend. North of Kirkintilloch the line skirted the Campsies, so you could travel by train to Aberfoyle, Balloch and Stirling – all lines which have gone now.

Kirkintilloch had one remarkable visitor in 1785: the Italian balloonist Vicenzo Lunardi took off from central Glasgow watched by a crowd estimated at 100,000. He landed north of Kirkintilloch, which practically emptied as people streamed out to see this marvel. A few kilometres from Lunardi's touch-down site is Antermony, where a more remarkable traveller was born in 1691. John Bell, a doctor, went to serve the Czar Peter I in 1714. From there he went to Persia (Iran) and later right across Russia to China – a 16-month journey. After further journeys in Turkey and Persia he became a merchant in Constantinople. He returned to Antermony about 1746, and wrote a book about his adventures. An unusual canal visitor in 1952 was the midget submarine XE IX, which spent the night in the Townhead, J & J Hay boatyard, since gone. (The puffer *Vital Spark* of the TV series was one built in the yard.)

Probably the town's most famous son was Tom Johnston – journalist, historian, politician, Secretary of State for Scotland, creator of the Highland hydro industry, and Chairman of the Scottish Council of the Forestry Commission and the Scottish Tourist Board (among other things). He was also a consummate politician and a member of Churchill's wartime cabinet. It was the war that led to his appointment as surely the best (some would say only) Secretary of State *for* Scotland, and out of the war, with shortages and difficulties, the Hydro Board was created to tap the Highland water for power, a fairly assured renewable energy resource.

Kirkintilloch is another place where water is fed into the canal to keep it operational, this time coming from the Johnstone, Woodend, Lochend and Bishops Lochs, well to the south.

16

Into the Heart of Glasgow
OSLR 64; OSE 342

We continue with Glasgow 11km (7mls) ahead and Falkirk 25km (15½mls) astern. Heading on from Kirki, the canal is first dominated by huge flats overlooking a very long staging (with a dry dock), a college campus, then the Seagull Trust boathouse (base for *Yarrow Seagull* and *Marjorie Seagull*) and the entrance to the Southbank Marina (council offices there) and an unusual boomerang-shaped footbridge by a new primary school.

Yarrow Seagull
approaching its
Kirkintilloch
boathouse

On the towpath side we pass St Ninian's High School then, across, lies Joe's Wharf with attendant boats no doubt. A wall marks the Park Burn overspill. A firm towpath through a rural landscape gives easy walking to Glasgow Road Bridge. A plaque on the wall below the bridge mentions it being opened in 1990 – the first of the Forth & Clyde Canal culverts to be replaced with a bridge so that canal navigation could be resumed. (The original was a swing bridge.) The bridge is concrete, but with attractive lines. The Stables was just that in olden days. Its modern status as a restaurant and pub may be welcome! The *Craft Daft on a Raft* also does teas etc. Do call in. Built in 1934, it was the Finnieston Ferry on the Clyde till 1977.

This is the main base for the Forth & Clyde Canal Society, whose boats are based here: the *Gipsy Princess, Janet Telford, Voyager* and the odd *Maryhill*. (Cruises, summer weekends and charters available.) Moving on, there is now a dock and launch slip opposite, though the earliest of these modern boats had to be lowered by crane!

The no longer clear Roman Wall line runs parallel to the A803, so the canal cuts it once more just east of Glasgow Road Bridge. The wall crosses back at Cadder, then keeps well north through Bearsden (the foundations of a bath-house on display) before a gradual descent to the Clyde at Old Kilpatrick. For many centuries it was called Graham's Dyke, or Grim's Dyke, just as Hadrian's Wall was the Picts' Wall. Archaeology is a young science.

The din of the A803 fades as the towpath wends westwards, a remarkably rural section, and the rural feel is maintained for a surprisingly long time, if pylons are ignored. The bridge on the Torrance road, Hungryside Bridge (a 'drawbridge' originally) is rather battered and repaired, but loved of cushie doos. And why the 'windows' in the abutments? There is a small car park. The Campsie Fells and the Kelvin valley fill the view to the north.

The canal twists and bends round to come on the staging and huts etc of a residential setting for boats. Cadder Church looms off right. (Cadder is pronounced Cawder.) In the kirkyard there is a mort safe and watch-house harking back to the days of the Resurrectionists; with prices for corpses higher in Edinburgh than in Glasgow, the canals came in useful!

An underground fire in Cadder No. 15 pit cost the lives of 22 miners in 1913. Two railway accidents are connected with the Cadder stretch of the Edinburgh–Glasgow line. In 1973, 50 yards of track were ripped up during a high-speed derailment, and ten years later passengers had to leap from the train as two coaches caught fire.

In the 18th century there arose a row in the Church of Scotland about patronage (more of which below). This involved a young lawyer who was

Cadder Church

an elder at Cadder Kirk, and whose family home at nearby Huntershill has made the name Muir of Huntershill one to remember. He suggested the idea – to us quite innocuous – that everyone should have a vote, and for his stand on such principles he was to be thrown into a life which, if written as fiction, would sound improbable.

Arrested for sedition and then released on bail, he went to France to try and plead with the Revolution leaders not to execute Louis XVI, as that would damage the cause of reform in Britain. The outbreak of war between Britain and France meant he was late back for his trial, so he was arrested and carried to Edinburgh in chains. In England he would probably soon have been free, but the grim Lord Braxfield sentenced him to 14 years' transportation, which was all too often a death sentence in disguise. Muir survived the horrendous voyage out to Australia and then escaped on an American ship which, after crossing the Pacific, was wrecked on the west coast of North America. He and one other survived, though the latter soon died.

Despite hostile Red Indians, Muir walked out of that situation, only to be arrested by the Spanish authorities in Central America. He was sent to Spain, but that ship was wrecked too. Fished out of the sea, he was taken to Cuba and then across the Atlantic to Cadiz, where the ship was engaged in a ferocious battle with an English frigate. Muir fought for the Spaniards as the lesser evil, and was severely wounded, losing the sight of one eye. Put ashore, he was eventually freed to travel to France where he lived out the rest of his short but eventful life. Muir was only 34 when he died.

Patronage simply meant that it was the local laird, not the congregation, who appointed the minister, an issue that divided Scotland for a century until the system was abolished. In Kirkintilloch, those who objected used to walk over the Campsies to church in Stirling each Sunday – a round trip of 35 miles! A Thomas Muir Heritage Trail has been made from his home, Huntershill (now swallowed up in Bishopbriggs), thence to Cadder, the canal on to Kirkintilloch and then by the Glazert Water to the Clachan of Campsie.

We don't see any more in the way of Roman remains, but stones from a fort were used on the canal banks here, and in several places objects were saved – four altars for instance were found at Auchendavy, near Kirkintilloch.

Cadder Bridge was once a drawbridge. The continuation feels spacious. Farm Bridge (No 24 Balmuildy Road) is next, and the canal continues its rural setting for several kilometres even though a convergence of power lines head to an electrical sub-station. Look out for a sign 'Possil Loch Circular Path 1¼k' which might appeal; it circuits extensive reed beds and comes out just before the next bridge at Lambhill (SWT board). Last time there, I watched a buzzard with a dead rabbit being harassed by magpies. In 1804 there was the whizz bang of a meteorite strike here. The largest piece of space rock is in the Hunterian Museum in Glasgow.

Lambhill Bridge carries the busy A879 to Milngavie (pron. Mill-guy) and just before it is another change house ('horse barracks'), long derelict and the site a scrapyard. Lambhill Stables is now an outdoor centre, offering canoe and cycle activities, has created a wonderful garden, and has organised allotments locally, all from local voluntary efforts. Regeneration at its best.

There is a small tearoom (Tues–Sun) and a striking memorial to the Cadder Pit disaster mentioned earlier: there are two bogies loaded with coal, and a clock set at the time the fatal shift went down. Identical barred tunnel entrances on each side of the canal are for the big Loch Katrine to Glasgow water supply pipeline which dives below the canal at this spot.

*The restored
Lambhill Stables*

An ice breaker on the Forth & Clyde Canal in earlier times (Campsie Fells *behind*)

The mile on to the Stockingfield Junction has plenty of bends, but, like the Union Canal, is following a single contour, that of the summit pound. There is a derelict wartime stop lock before the unobtrusive junction. The towpath now swops sides so one has to descend, go through the road tunnel (Lochburn Road) and up the other side (sloping paths, both sides). An oval marker indicates 2½mls to Spiers Wharf on the Glasgow Branch and 9¼mls to Bowling. An 1898 OS map indicated a wee ferry to avoid this down and up. The canal also brought farm produce into Glasgow – from as far away as Grangemouth on the Firth of Forth. In 1830 the canal company introduced cart boats, onto which horse and cart could be loaded – a sort of roll-on-roll-off service!

While noisily urban at times (heavy traffic off-stage) the going remains as rural as ever, and the Glasgow Branch runs high, so there are views over rooftops and streets to spires and towers. A dismantled railway passes below, then a three-arched overspill is passed and a bend leads to Ruchill Street Bridge which, like the Firhill Bridge ahead, had to be rebuilt in MM style after the years of being culverted. A basin (now filled in) once served the Bryant and May match factory, which has also disappeared. Ruchill Church on the right, built of red sandstone, has an adjoining hall built earlier, designed by Rennie Mackintosh. It now faces a McDonalds! Across the bridge are one-time rubber works built in period brick, which are listed buildings and slowly being restored for other uses. Many other old buildings have disappeared, though, but many attractive flats are going up. After stagings on our side and then on the other there are very colourful flats.

Bilsland Drive Aqueduct (1879) sees traffic pass unobtrusively (unless you peer over the parapet) under the canal, which then makes a big loop with busy Maryhill Road below on the right. A footbridge connects with modern housing. Firhill Road bridge (Nolly Bridge) rises across the canal to run up to Ruchill Park and, off left from it, the sweep of the Murano Street tenements (1899–1903) are a classic survivor. Abutments once led onto what is now an island – and a valuable wildlife sanctuary. The canal twists and turns. From here to Port Dundas there are facilities for exercising on the apparatus of a 'Trim Trail'. In the crook of the loop lies Firhill Park, home of Partick Thistle Football Club (the Jags). Partick Thistle first played on a public ground, where Kelvingrove now stands (1876). Big

In Glasgow – but would you know it? (from the Nolly Bridge)

Old works restored, on the Glasgow Branch of the Forth & Clyde Canal

1888 development forced a move, and there were four more moves before the Jags landed at Firhill in 1909.

At Queen's Cross, on the other side of the stadium, is an 1899 Mackintosh church, his first ecclesiastical work, now the home of the Charles Rennie Mackintosh Society. The Firhill Basins lying on the outer side of the loop were once busy timber yards. Much of the timber was from Scandinavia and was brought through the canal from Grangemouth. Timber basins were used for seasoning the wood in water so, as you can imagine, were notorious for causing fatalities among children, who could not resist playing at 'rafts' and would swim whenever supervision was absent. The canal drowned the careless. There's a story of one local who became quite a hero and was awarded medals for leaping in to rescue people, until it came out that he was getting a mate to push them into the water in the first place. There were other fatalities when the canals froze and people fell through the ice. This freezing could halt traffic, another reason the coming of the railways would see canal use decline. The Murano name may come from the island near Venice, as glassmaking was also a one-time Firhill industry, sand being another product carried on the canal.

There is plenty of staging here, but sadly, nobody is going to leave a boat unprotected in these parts. Here too, in World War II, another stop lock was added in case enemy bombing breached the canal (which would have been disastrous for much of the city below) so the canal was carefully portioned off into safer volumes of water.

The canal swings gradually left. Across, inset into Hamilton Hill, is an abandoned basin which was once a clay quarry, source of material for lining the canals. A green-painted tin pigeon loft is all that points to a once popular activity along the canal. The university is well seen, and all the city spires and towers. A wide section of towpath leads us to the oval-shaped Hamiltonhill Basin, with a cluster of boats moored along the enclosure of Scottish Canals HQ. This was the original (1777) terminus of the Glasgow Branch. There's an obvious stop lock and a row of workshops, and working boats for dredging weed and all the junk that gets tipped into the canals. The slip at the office block was the first on the canal, where the company built and serviced its boats.

A lane heads down, right, leading to Garscube Road, under the M8 and so into the city centre, a 15-minute walk. Rockvilla Bridge, a bascule

*A Dutch barge beside the Scottish
Canals Head Quarters, Hamiltonhill*

bridge, of the style to be met frequently on the Bowling section of the canal, leads across to the Scottish Canals site on Applecross Street, the street coming in off Possil Road, which goes under the canal and down to the M8, the last major aqueduct. The Possil Road aqueduct dates to 1880, but the original 1790 Whitworth Aqueduct, which is 'seduced' (superseded) is easy to overlook. It comes first; a curved wall. There are facilities for four residential moorings. It is worthwhile dropping down to street level to look at the massive stonework of the aqueduct, similar to those of Bilsland, Lochburn and Maryhill. There was another stop lock at the canal's HQ, but the footbridge has a clever method of opening to allow boats' passage: half the bridge can slide back alongside the other half.

A last bend (once another timber yard), and the canal comes to the impressive reach of Spiers Wharf, for many years the end of the city branch of the canal. Notable restoration work has been done on what, a century ago, were thriving sugar works, grain mills, breweries and bonded warehouses, some seven storeys high. (The back walls, out of sight, are only brick!) At the far end is an elegant porticoed Georgian building of 1812 which was the original Forth & Clyde Canal Company offices. The Swifts departed from here for Falkirk (and, from 1822 with the Union opening, to Edinburgh) and later it was the city base for the pleasure craft plying out to rural Craigmarloch. Over 2005–06 the section from Hamiltonhill to Spiers Wharf was drained in order to survey the fabric, the first inspection of the walls built over 200 years ago. They had been built well. When the canal was pushed on to Bowling, this branch was also extended.

From Spiers Wharf the canal turned east to reach Port Dundas, a series of basins, a very real port in the heart of the city. From below there was the strange sight of crowded ships' masts against the sky. Because of changes since the canals closed, it was no longer possible to recreate the connection as it was – but this problem was solved ingeniously: a lock drops down to a large kidney-shaped basin (moorings galore), with the M8 alongside, then goes under a road to a second lock back up – and so to Port Dundas: a £7 million outlay.

Pedestrians, perforce, go up steps to cross this road (right, it drops under the M8 for the city centre) and continue along to reach a swing bridge which once took the railway into the thriving docks, then there is a bascule footbridge which we cross (note the barge on the green) to walk round the dock's rim. The big Pinkston Watersports Centre which has every facility imaginable, including a white-water canoe course, occupies a basin in the centre area, which is otherwise just planted with trees (birch). Walk

Constructing the new lock beside the M8 in Glasgow to restore access to Port Dundas

along to the far corner where there is an intake for topping up the water level – which comes from the culverted waters of the one-time Monkland Canal, described in Appendix 3. Sadly, some of the plans for regenerating Port Dundas have stalled. There are no flats looking over a plaza where we could sit to celebrate our travels. Pity about the litter. Mind you, at its peak the area was 'resounding with the noise of manufactories and the hum of industry' (*Companion*), with some of the tallest chimneys in the world pouring out smoke and fumes.

The name Port Dundas commemorates one of the major backers of the canal, Sir Lawrence Dundas, a merchant who had made his money selling stores to HM Forces, owned estates and interests at Grangemouth and elsewhere, and had made a killing out of the resulting developments. He cut the first sod at Grangemouth in 1768. To recap: by 1773 ships could operate to Kirkintilloch, by 1775 to Stockingfield; and by 1777 the Glasgow Branch was operational as far as Hamiltonhill. However funds had run out, and it was 1784 before a government advance came through. In 1786 operations commenced to push the main line through to Bowling, and everything was operational in 1790.

The canal as a human transport facility came more slowly. The world's first practical steamer, the *Charlotte Dundas*, was introduced in 1801, and in 1828 the *Cyclops* (based on a Mississippi steamboat) was tried, but both

Swing bridge and bascule bridge at the entrance to Port Dundas

damaged the banks. The twin-hulled *Swift* came in then, but it was 1831 before design and function succeeded with the *Rapid*, the first of a whole series of 'Swifts' with names like *Velocity, Gazelle, Dart, Gleam* and *Swallow*. A cabin, with entertainment and comforts, was a big advance on carriage travel. The *Charlotte Dundas* eventually became the canal's first steam dredger, and operated as such for many years.

In 1875, George Aitken began a goods and passenger service between Port Dundas and Castlecary (a one-legged fiddler entertained), but Aitken was drowned in the canal a few years after. His son James launched the *Fairy Queen* 13 years later, and it, and its companions and successors, became immensely popular. An advertisement in 1916 offered a whole day's excursion: sail, dinner in the Bungalow at Craigmarloch, time ashore, 'dainty' afternoon tea on deck or in the saloon, all for four shillings and three pence (equivalent to about £82 now). Dinner at Craigmarloch cost two shillings (about £40). The service lasted till World War II, when the *Gypsy Queen* headed in the other direction, to Dalmuir, to be broken up.

The canal itself never recovered from the war, and in 1963 was officially closed. It rapidly suffered vandalism and dumping and, with fatalities, voices were raised to fill it in. Happily, at the last moment, its worth as a leisure asset became better understood and, ever since, slowly and determinedly, it has been brought back to life.

In 1793 the Monkland Canal was linked to Port Dundas, built largely to make cheap Lanarkshire coal available to the city – 80,000 tons of it in 1808. The Monkland 'water' was a useful bonus for topping up the Glasgow Branch and also the descent to the Clyde – and, technically, also heading to the Forth from Wyndford Lock. I have been told that fish marked at Bowling have turned up in Edinburgh.

James Watt was the surveyor and first engineer of this project which entailed 18 locks and had an inclined plane at Blackhill, up which empty boats were hauled to gain 30m (100ft), save time, and reduce water loss through the locks. The canal closed to traffic in 1935 and there is no likelihood of any restoration; much of it is under the M8. The Airdrie–Coatbridge area was the centre of Scotland's steel industry which has disappeared, but the region has slowly rejuvenated itself. A few stretches of the canal can still be seen and walked, and highly recommended is a visit to Coatbridge's Summerlee Museum of Scottish Industrial Life, a superlative site for this historical area with ironworks, sawmill, and mining displays, trams and a tramway – and a replica of the *Vulcan*, the world's first iron-hulled ship. More on this canal in Appendix 3.

17

Down to the Clyde: Maryhill to Bowling

OSLR 64; OSE 342

Soon after leaving the Stockingfield Junction, the busy Maryhill Road is crossed, with a view to several towers, and a church below. Stark modern flats with towpath-edging shrubs lead on to Lock 21, the start of the Maryhill flight of locks. The building beside Lock 21 is an old inn. Lock 21 is the western end of the summit pound that we have followed ever since Wyndford Lock, what feels a long time ago! Maryhill Road runs beside the canal at this point, and there is staging and a slip before Lock 21. There is still the Kelvin Dock pub across Maryhill Road, however, and a pub called 'Lock 27' not far ahead. The name Maryhill comes from an heiress, Mary Hill, who freed land for development with the condition her name was commemorated. Chemical works, timber yards, metal fabrications and ship building developed.

The Maryhill Locks form perhaps the most spectacular flight on the Lowland canals as it drops from the summit level, Lock 21, to Lock 25 with the Kelvin Aqueduct just beyond, and big ink-blot shaped basins between each drop and historic Kelvin Dock lying off at right angles from Lock 22. Kelvin Dock was operational from 1789 to 1949, the oldest yard on the canal, where canal company boats were launched, both sideways and stern first; and there was also a dry dock. Inscribed on a dockside path are the names of boats launched there.

The smaller barges were called 'scows' (perhaps from the Dutch *schouw*, a flat-bottom boat) and the large barges were 'lighters'. Most notably, here the first-ever 'puffer' was built (the *Glasgow*), a type of coastal cargo vessel immortalised in the Para Handy stories of Neil Munro. The puffer evolved from the scow, which was towed by horses till engines came along. Landing craft for the D-Day landings in World War II were one of the last projects undertaken in the docks. Naval ships have not been great canal users, though the miniature submarine in 1952 caused some interest.

Crossing the Kelvin Aqueduct. (The impressive view is from below)

The four-arched Kelvin Aqueduct, built in 1790, and then the largest project of such a nature in Britain, is still impressive. Seaton having retired, Robert Whitworth was the engineer called to take the canal the 130m (400ft) across the 22m (70ft) deep River Kelvin valley. The technology of the times necessitated the aqueduct's massive strength, whereas the 'great three' of the Union Canal (Avon, Slateford, Almond) were able to use newer skills to produce more slender structures. The cost was £8,500, against an estimate of £6,200, so over-running is nothing new, though more justified with such a pioneering feat which brought tourists by their thousand – and inspired plenty of well-forgotten poetic odes! One history of Glasgow enthuses, 'uniting the German and Atlantic Oceans … squared rigged vessels are sometimes seen navigating 70 feet above spectators … a pre-eminence over everything of a similar nature in the Kingdom'.

The Kelvin Walkway runs below the aqueduct, linking Kelvingrove with the West Highland Way. At the east end of the aqueduct a path (with steps) drops down to gain the walk/cycleway. The great strength of the aqueduct is best seen from below despite the choking of trees (winter is a good time to see it), and a return should be made by the same route to continue along the canal. The Glasgow Botanic Garden, University, Kelvingrove Museum and Art Gallery, Kelvingrove Park and the Hunterian Museum can all be reached downstream by the walkway.

Considering the canal is in the middle of a city, the scenery and setting remains remarkably rural. The first bridge, Govan Cottage Bridge, was rebuilt as part of the restoration in the Millennium style. Kelvindale Station lies above the bridge. Walking on, the view is dominated by the two Temple gasometers which the towpath passes. There are signs of old mineral line crossings, and Lock 26 has current railway tunnels passing underneath just to east and west. Lock 27 is interesting. An original bascule bridge carried the Crow Road (North) over the canal here at Temple, but in 1932 the Bearsden Road was realigned and a huge steel lifting bridge installed. This has since gone and there is now a sturdy four-lane iron girder bridge. A model of the lifting bridge is in the Museum of Scotland in Edinburgh (Chambers Street). A footbridge crosses the canal just west of Lock 27.

'Lock 27' is a popular public house, and is on the site of an original lock-keeper's cottage, with plenty of outside seating beside the canal. You can

A timber yard in the heart of Glasgow in the canal's heyday. (By Lock 27; the lifting bridge now the A739 Bearsden Road)

take your pick for the distance to Bowling; one sign says 7¾ miles, another 8½. Here and on the stretch ahead new housing has been developed on the site of the once-busy timber yards, timber brought from across the North Sea and through Grangemouth.

Continuing, you pass under the massive iron bridge with red sandstone abutments, the busy Bearsden Road. Beyond there is staging and facilities for canal boats, kept locked out of necessity.

Attractive houses face the canal and a utilitarian but graceful concrete bridge serves the Lynch Estate. The delightful Netherton swing bridge lies beside houses in a style more often seen in the south of England. One time I was here a cormorant went winging past. Gentle suburbia continues, with houses ranged above the railway on the right. The Westerton footbridge, the next landmark, a single girder bridge with a twirl down at the south end, leads to Westerton station, and stations from here to Bowling can make useful returns from the parts of canal walked.

Another attractive flight of locks, 28–32, Clobberhill, leads to a footbridge with the Blairdardie playing fields to the right and a pleasant tree area to walk through on our side. There is a big, new double concrete road bridge for the Great Western Road. The historic Bard Avenue bascule bridge has a wee shop close by.

The long stretch of the Boghouse Locks, 33–36, give a last flight, with only three more locks to come before meeting the sea. (There is a footbridge at Lock 35.) Much had to be rebuilt in this area to reopen the canal. Lock 36 had to be re-instated, hence the odd kink in the western approach to it. Duntreath Avenue Bridge is another big concrete structure connecting Yoker and Drumchapel, where we begin to be aware of the Kilpatrick Hills. The bridge was culverted before the millennium restoration. In Victorian times this was pleasant countryside, Drumchapel a holiday destination. After the Linvale bascule bridge there are long straights leading to the Clyde Shopping Park. One stretch of canal was kept for its amenity value but was reduced to a couple of feet deep 'for safety'.

Before Bridge 40, the old-style oval distance marker notes: 6¼km to Bowling, 45½km to Falkirk. On the other side of the bridge is the canal institution of McMonagles *Debra Rose* floating chip restaurant, with (at the time of writing) a unique 'sail through' service.

Clyde Shopping Park with all the big names present is a canal novelty; the canal sails through the middle of it. A Victorian bandstand looks a bit marooned. There is a stark big church. And to keep pedestrians on the move along the Sylvania Way there are two footbridges, the western with a stylish

Through the Clyde Shopping Centre

canopy; both can lift to allow boats through – but one at a time so there is no interruption for shoppers. This is a prime example of a development centring on the canal, thanks to West Dunbartonshire Council.

Clydebank was devastated by wartime bombing, when 4,000 homes were destroyed (only eight escaped undamaged), with heavy civilian casualties, and the steady decline in shipbuilding has done little for morale; gone are the days when ships like the *Lusitania*, *Queen Mary* and *QE2* towered beside the Clyde. We are made aware of Glasgow Airport across the river; memories of the miles out of Edinburgh on the Union Canal.

The Kilbowie Road Bridge, as we leave, had to be rebuilt as it was previously culverted. The north side of the canal has a high concrete wall running along to an abutment of an old bridge. A railway runs alongside on the left, with a branch bearing off into the docks, and this soon passes below the canal, the tunnel only noted from the towpath as there is a brick wall. The view along the line leads the eye back to the cranes of Clydebank. The huge Singer Sewing Machine Factory lay north of here, now a modern industrial estate. In its heyday the factory's cooling water flowing into the canal supported a thriving number of goldfish. At the height of its success over a million sewing machines were produced in a year. The works closed in 1980.

Shortly after, the canal crosses a minor road. A sloping path/steps descend onto Boquharan Road. It is worth going down to see two things: the unusual narrow brick bridge with its raised pedestrian way (really a

The one-time Singer Sewing Machine Factory, Clydebank (closed 1980)

pend), and out across the Dumbarton Road, left, on the wall above the Park Tavern, is an interesting carved feature showing a First World War battleship. Shops on Dumbarton Road may be welcome, and one can follow the road along to Dalmuir in a few minutes.

Trafalgar Street pedestrian bridge (all metal mesh) comes next, an area favoured by swans. One October I spent an enjoyable time watching them from the bridge as they indulged in vigorous preening, often rolling over upside down in the water and flapping violently, the cygnets testing out their new-discovered powers of flight. Asters still gave a touch of blue on the green banks, while the trees of this very woody stretch were lighting up with autumn colours.

One of the most ingenious tricks of the Millennium Link comes next: the Dalmuir 'Drop Lock'. Originally a bascule bridge had sufficed on the Dumbarton Road, but later there was a sturdy swing bridge across which tramcars clanked. Both trams and canal ceased to function in the sixties, Glasgow's very last tram was the No 9 Auchenshuggle to Dalmuir West.

Such a major road across the canal line set problems, the solution being to create a lock that could lower boats under the obstruction and then raise them again – the first such lock of this kind in Britain; nothing distinctly different to look at, but brilliant. Note the Beardmore sculpture – also of a battleship.

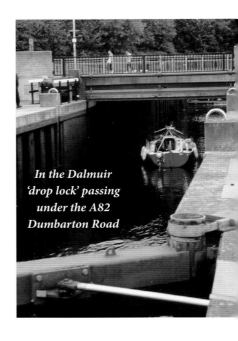

In the Dalmuir 'drop lock' passing under the A82 Dumbarton Road

Continuing, there is Farm Road bascule bridge, with huge high pylons crossing the view, for they span the River Clyde. From the large 1934 Erskine swing bridge, a road leads down to where the ferry operated across the Clyde before the bridge opened (1865–1971). In the 19th century a ferryboat could carry up to 40 head of cattle and was pulled across on a chain. Now, as one guide puts it, the bridge is 'elegant in the distant landscape but awesomely monstrous above the village'. Ironically, this last section (almost as level as the Union Canal) was soon made unnecessary by the Clyde being regularly dredged to allow seagoing ships up into the city. Had practical dredging come earlier, the Forth & Clyde canal might have had locks through the city below Port Dundas to reach the Clyde.

Down that ferry road is the entrance to The Saltings, a nature reserve, where there is a description board and car park, the site dominated by the great bridge. One can exit from the reserve back to the towpath 200 yards west of the swing bridge. From the swing bridge, about the same distance along the main road is the village cluster of shops, post office, coffee bar and the Glen Lusset Restaurant. The restored Lock 37 lies just west of the swing bridge and almost under the Erskine Bridge.

Old Kilpatrick's church tower is a landward mark. The wartime blitz has left some of the gravestones pitted, chipped or repaired from enemy machine gun fire. The canal here cut through the bath-house of a Roman fort. Ferrydyke bascule bridge is the only break in a 1.5km stretch of canal. A bridge-keeper's cottage is now ruinous. Nearby was the western terminal fort of the Roman Antonine Wall, which descended to the Clyde here after its sweep across Scotland from the Forth. There is an aptness in the two great engineering feats, almost two millennia apart, marching across the country so companionably. Does the Ferrydyke name commemorate this?

On a winter walk this way I once watched two young swans fly in to land on the canal; they presumed it was water and it was only when they put down their big feet that they discovered the canal was frozen solid. The sight of swans sliding along on their bottoms, on their necks, and round and round reduced spectators to hysterics. The attractive Kilpatrick Hills are close to the canal now, and a railing shows where a burn, coming off the slopes, passes under the canal. Suddenly you come on the final features of the canal, starting with a busy marina in a large basin. Look out for the *Wee Spark*, a miniature puffer.

Lock 38, below the white house, leads into a big high-walled basin, also well used, with a last bascule bridge at its end before the Forth & Clyde canal goes under the once-operational Caledonian Railway swing bridge (Lock 39) to the boat-crowded last basin itself. This can be busy, and in winter many boats are moored there for the season with the yachties busy working on them at weekends, always a very attractive scene. It took 22 years for the canal to reach Bowling (in 1790). I trust we've had a less fraught experience on our journey across Scotland.

Circumambulating the basin you come onto an overspill, which was once the original sea lock. Between two and five million gallons of water flows through the Forth & Clyde canal system each day. The view upriver is always fine, with the Erskine Bridge seen at its best. There's a Millennium Link monument and a wood carving of a squirrel. The point on the other side of the overspill gives a good view to the large, but unused, Bowling harbour. The mighty River Clyde is surprisingly narrow; hard to imagine great liners or battleships passing. On the point of Bowling harbour is a monument to Henry Bell, of the *Comet* steamship fame. (The *Comet* was wrecked on Craignish Point in 1820 while operating a Glasgow–Fort William service through the Crinan Canal.)

Continuing, there is just the sea lock to cross. Your canal walk is over. To celebrate the opening of the full canal in 1790, a hogshead of Forth water was poured into the Clyde. Your celebrations will no doubt be more modest.

The way out passes the toilet/shower block and goes left of the lawn leading to the 18th-century Customs House, and along by the old railway to reach the bascule bridge. From it a road heads up and over the busy railway line to reach the Bowling road (A814). Across the road there is a bus stop for buses back to Clydebank/Glasgow, a service operating about

Bowling Basin with the old Customs House

every quarter of an hour. For trains, a ten-minute walk west along the main road leads to the station. A car park is passed on the way, overlooking the Old Bowling Basin, and visiting cars should be parked here, not down by the canal basin.

The *Companion* again: 'there are few foreign landscapes whose beauties really excel those of the scenes just described. There are few landscapes that unite the cultivated charms, rural scenery, and lofty mountain grandeur, which are so finely blended on the Forth & the Clyde.'

APPENDICES

1

Canal Code

Good manners and friendliness are the basics to ensure safety on canal towpaths. Think of other users. Follow the Country Code, and see it as a charter of freedom, not a restriction.

Canal byelaws do not allow horse-riding, motorbike or vehicle use of the towpath. This is obviously in the interests of safety as well as enjoyment.

Cyclists should take care not to startle walkers and MUST warn when approaching from behind. Treat aqueducts and locks with great care, as indeed should pedestrians, who should also let fishermen know of their approach. Anglers should be careful not to interfere with other users. Beware of overhead power lines.

A Ratho sculpture

Close all gates. There is nothing calculated to annoy farmers more than having to round up strayed livestock. Don't go over walls, or through fences or hedges. There are always gates or stiles where needed on our route. Leave livestock, crops, boats and machinery alone. Guard against all risk of fires.

Dump your litter in bins, not in the countryside or the canal. You'll see some sad sights. Don't add to them. Poly bags can mean death to a grazing cow, broken glass is wicked for both man and beast, drink bottles and cans are an insufferable eyesore and dog poo bags are not the best decoration for canalside trees.

Walk quietly in the countryside. Nature goes unobtrusively and you should too. Collect memories, not specimens.

Dogs need strict control and should not be allowed to foul the towpath.

2

Canal Contacts

These are contacts for most of the more established canal bodies and facilities. Venues can close down or change opening hours, so it is advisable to check beforehand – and I will welcome information on any changes; you can contact me via Whittles Publishing by email on info@whittlespublishing.com.

Accommodation can be booked at the Visit Scotland centres in Edinburgh, Linlithgow, Falkirk Wheel (none in Falkirk), Glasgow and Dumbarton. (Listed below.)

General	
Almondell & Calderwood Country Park	01506 882 254 almondell&calderwood@west-lothian.gov.uk
Almond Valley Heritage Centre	01506 414 957
Annet House, Linlithgow (museum)	01506 670 677 www.annethousemuseum.org.uk
Antonine Wall	www.antonineway.com; www.antoninewall.org
Beecraigs Country Park	01506 844 516 www.beecraigs.com
Beefeater, Rosebank (Camelon)	01324 611 842
Boat hirings – see end of listings	
Boathouse (by Kilsyth)	01236 829 200
Bridge Inn, Ratho	0131 333 1320 www.bridgeinn.com
Cairnpapple Hill (Historic Scotland)	0131 550 7603
Callendar House/Park	01324 503 770 www.falkirkcommunitytrust.org
Craft Daft on a Raft (Glasgow Bridge)	0791 086 0225 www.craftdaftonaraft.co.uk
Cycle Hire (Outdoor Trax)	07828 008 997
Debra Rose (chippy)	0141 951 1333/2444
Drumpellier Country Park	www.northlanarkshire.gov.uk
Edinburgh Canal Society (rowing boats)	07806 461 996
EICA (Edinburgh International Climbing Arena)	0131 333 6333 www.eica-ratho.co.uk
Falkirk Wheel	08700 500 208 www.thefalkirkwheel.co.uk
Forth & Clyde Canal Society	01236 735 533 www.forthandclyde.org.uk

General	
Geo Projects (Canals map)	0118 939 3567
Helix (park)	01324 590 900 www.thehelix.co.uk
Historic Scotland	0131 668 8600 www.historic-Scotland.gov.uk
John Muir Way	www.johnmuirway.org
Linlithgow Palace	01506 842 896
Lock 27 (restaurant)	0141 958 0853
LUCS (Linlithgow Union Canal Society) Museum, tearoom, etc	01506 843 194/01506 671 215 www.lucs.org.uk
Muir, Thomas	www.thomasmuir.co.uk
Muiravonside Country Park	01506 845 311 www.falkirkcommunitytrust.org
Pinkerton Water Sports	0141 433 8636
St Michael's Church, Linlithgow	01506 842 188
Scottish Canals (British Waterways Scotland), Canal House, Applecross Street, Glasgow G4 9SP	0141 332 6936 www.scottishcanals.co.uk
Scottish Waterways Trust (volunteering)	01324 677 822 www.scottishwaterwaystrust.org.uk
Stables, The (Glasgow Bridge)	0141 777 6088
Summerlee (Museum)	www.visitlanarkshire.com/summerlee
Sustrans	0845 113 0065 www.sustrans.org.uk
Tally Ho Inn, Winchburgh	01506 890 221
Traveline Scotland	0871 200 2233 www.travelinescotland.com
Union Inn (Lock 16)	01324 626 697
Visit Scotland Tourist Offices:	
Dumbarton	01389 763 444
Edinburgh	0131 473 3800
Falkirk Wheel	01324 620 244
Glasgow	0141 204 4400
Linlithgow	01506 844 600 (Apr–Sept)
Water of Leith Visitor Centre	0131 455 7367
Boat Hiring, Cruising	
Major operators:	
Capercaillie Cruisers	01324 627 212
Alvechurch Boat Centres	0330 3330 590
Black Prince Holidays	01527 575 115
Marine Cruises	01244 373 911

General	
Others noted:	
Chartered Hotel Boat	07702 242 160
Re-union Day Boat Hire	0131 261 8529
ABC Boat Hire	0330 333 0590
Ratho Inn (restaurant boats)	0131 333 1320
By Winchburgh: Bridge 19–40 Canal Society	01506 417 685 www.bridge19-40.org.uk
Edinburgh Canal Society	07806 461 996
Forth & Clyde Canal Society	0141 772 1620 www.forthandclyde.org.uk

SEAGULL TRUST

The Seagull Trust runs boats for disabled visitors, and a short one-hour trip for the general public at the Falkirk Wheel.

UC – Ratho: *Mackay Seagull, St John Crusader II*	0131 335 3318 www.stcruises-ratho.org.uk
UC – Falkirk (Bantaskine Park): *Govan Seagull, Barr Seagull*	07722 342 913 www.stcruises-falkirk.org.uk
F&CC – Falkirk Wheel: *Marion Seagull, Wooden Spoon Seagull.* Operated by Seagull Enterprises and, as well a school and other charitable work may be chartered for cruising, corporate use, etc.	07513 291 792 www.seagulltrust.org.uk
F&CC – Kirkintilloch. *Yarrow Seagull, Marjorie Seagull*	0141 777 7165 www.stcruises-kirkintilloch.org.uk

3

The Monkland Canal
OSLR 64; OSE 343

The Monkland Canal starts at a weir on the North Calder Water at Calderbank, south of Airdrie (NS 763624), and today runs for 2.5km before a culvert takes it through Coatbridge for 3.5km, to reappear (NS 721649) for a 2km section with a final barrier at NS 704640. The river's origins are no more than 3km short of Slamannan and the infant Union Canal's Avon. Hillhead is the main reservoir feeder. There are odd extension basin remnants, notably at the Summerlees museum, a good place to visit first as it can provide leaflets on local circular walks which can be combined with towpath wanderings. From Summerlee, the North Calder Heritage Trail (NCHT) follows the route of the canal through Coatbridge and then the towpath to the dam at Calderbank (and on to the Hillhead reservoir). The other remnant western section is equally accessible from the Summerlee museum. Considering the enclosing urban world, the walking is completely countrified, the distant thrum of traffic the only intrusion.

Start the CALDERBANK walk at Summerlee museum, following the NCHT signs through the town (on the line of the culvert) to reach a minor road (a western extension of the B802). The canal is signed across the road; the culverting point is given some decoration, and immediately after there is a long, raised walkway for an overspill. Along the way there are three farm-road bridges and a pipeline which stalks right across the valley on high stilts; there are decorative seats, NCHT signs and information posts, including one at Faskine where the *Vulcan* was launched. From the last bridge the canal is very overgrown. The dam creates a small curtain waterfall. Paths lead up into Calderbank. On a sharp dewy morning along here I asked a fisherman what he hoped to catch. The reply was, 'Breakfast'. Unlike the Union Canal or Forth & Clyde Canal you can actually see the water here 'flowing'.

Leaving Summerlee by Heritage Way the WESTERN stretch of canal lies along by West Canal Street, kept as a walk and becoming very clear

A peaceful Monkland Canal remnant

as a bank along West End Park where the canal bursts forth, runs below a busy road (Blair Road) and on through attractive countryside. (Up on Blair Road there is a fine sculpted arch.) Drumpellier Country Park lies on the north side of the canal; at the start there is a slip and staging for access to the water. Part way along a footbridge gives access to the park. Hard to imagine this water reaching Bowling (or the Kelpies) and harder still to imagine these remnants crowded by the powerhouse of Scotland: five of the six biggest ironworks lay by the Monkland. A railway brings the practical walking to an end and the canal vanishes once more. A viewing boardwalk with attractive railings (designed in local schools) marks the spot. Cross, and return to the north side through Drumpellier Park. (Drumpellier Golf Course lies on the south side.)

The SUMMERLEE Museum of Scottish Industrial Life (opened in 1988) was the site of one major ironworks which operated from 1836 to 1926. The museum is one of Scotland's finest, its heart a vast exhibition hall covering everything industrial in a score of displays, including the working Cardowan winding engine, and a reproduction blast furnace. Upstairs is a large historical collection of cycles and an extension viewing pavilion which looks over the unique excavated site of the steelworks. There is a café where one can sit and watch the trams go by (or ride on one); there is the huge

Summerlee Museum of Scottish Industrial Life

Garrett loco, timber and sawmill buildings, a coal mine, miners' rows, etc. The site is embraced by a marooned bit of side canal (Gartsherrie Branch) with a basin (Howe's Basin), to recall how vital canals were. (Other side branches went to Calder, Dundyran and Langloan.)

The 1987 reproduction *Vulcan* is displayed here. Built in 1819 by Thomas Wilson, the original was the first *iron* craft afloat. He, and it, were scorned by sceptics who saw it sinking at once, but *Vulcan* stayed afloat for 60 years, pulled by two horses, carrying passengers (capacity 200) on the Forth & Clyde Canal, and later general heavy goods. All this sits in the heart of Coatbridge, a few minutes' walk from the town centre, a remarkable survival and new development, very much part of the canals' story.

Acknowledgements

This is largely written as it was for the original edition, with additions; but sadly, some people mentioned are no longer with us and many questioned on site remain anonymous. A special debt to Scottish Canals (previously British Waterways Scotland) is acknowledged, many of whose staff answered queries and, in the case of the Chief Engineer George Ballinger, brought the then new link from Spiers Wharf to Port Dundas to life for me. The Foreword by Andrew Thin, Chairman, Scottish Canals, is much appreciated. Other staff, past and present, I must mention are Jill Richards, Helen Rowbotham and Cara Baillie. Other enthusiastic experts who helped are canal historian Guthrie Hutton, Anne Street, Ronnie Rusack, Mel and Judy Gray (and successors at LUCS), Bill and Sandra Purves and many from the Seagull Trust. Thanks also to Don Martin and others at the William Patrick Library, Kirkintilloch, and the Edinburgh City Library, and to Jill, who walked some wintry days, to Kay and Iain and Heather and Peter, who ferried me to and from some of the days spent surveying and who offered hospitality overnight, to Richard and Edith Cormack for checking text, to Sheila Gallimore, who typed my notes so effectively and those at Whittles who took on the practicalities of publishing the guide.

All facts have been checked as far as possible, but neither the author nor the publisher can be held responsible for any errors, however caused, or for the use to which the guide is put. Developments and changes occur continuously, and the publisher would welcome information for correcting and updating any future edition.

INDEX

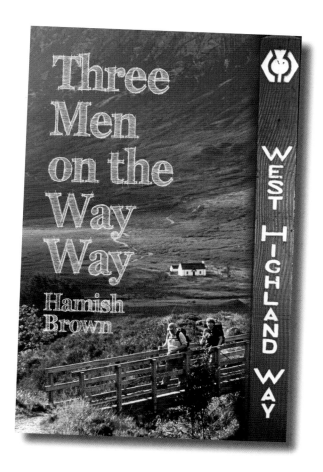

- …Hamish Brown captures the atmosphere the walk generates, and many readers will identify their trip with their own personal experiences of the Way. *The Scots Magazine*

- …This is not to be missed if you're planning your own adventure down this legendary trail. *The Great Outdoors*

available from
www.whittlespublishing.com

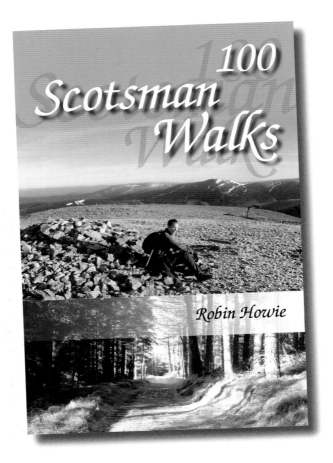

- ...The narrative which accompanies each of the walks makes for entertaining reading. ...Usefully divided into different areas, with full page maps at the start of each section, this is a book to inspire walkers and to delight the armchair traveller too. *Scottish Home & Country*

- ...The appeal in the book for me was the other walks which make up the bulk of the content. These give alternatives to Munros and Corbetts: ideal for half days and taking visitors perhaps not used to hillwalking. ... this book is ideal. *Munro Society Newsletter*

available from
www.whittlespublishing.com

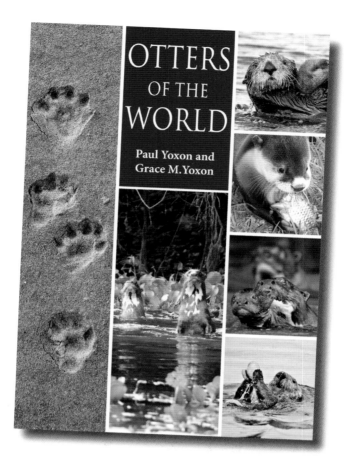

- ...contains a wealth of information regarding the status of all 13 species of otters worldwide. A gem of a book written with great affection by authors who have a deep understanding of their subject. *ECOS*

- The first book providing spectacular photographs and an insight into the lives and behaviour of ALL 13 species of otters... Beautifully illustrated with first class images ... an introduction to the magical world of otters, with many photos, distribution maps, and more. *Focusing on Wildlife blog*

 available from
www.whittlespublishing.com